POINTERS TO HEAVEN

John Twisleton

ISBN-13: 9798638091811
ISBN-10: 1477123456

Cover design by: Art Painter
Library of Congress Control Number: 2018675309
Printed in the United States of America

CONTENTS

PREFACE

I'm writing a preface to another preface. Christian faith sees earthly life as a preface to the book of real life. That life people first gained sight of through an event recorded in history no historian can fully evaluate, the death and resurrection of Jesus.

This book is an invitation to see earthly life as preface to the fuller life of heaven. To this fullness of life Jesus is supreme pointer but as I've reflected on my life experience I have come to identify ten pointers that should trouble anyone taking a purely material view of life.

I would be troubled by goodness, truth and beauty other than as pointers to attainable perfection, by love, suffering and visions which point to fulfilment beyond this world and by holy people who give us a taste of that realm.

If heaven makes sense of earth it does through such pointers, complemented by those revealed by God in the promises of scripture, the resurrection of Jesus and worship, which, in the eucharist, provides both a pointer to and preview of the life of the world to come. My namesake John the Baptist is patron of this book since he lived to point beyond himself to his Lord. May the stories I tell, the arguments I put, the scriptures I quote point beyond my text to the living word of the living God whose eternal company is promised to believers.

John Twisleton   Easter 2020

POINTERS TO HEAVEN
- 1 GOODNESS

Acts of kindness anticipating the communion of saints

Mrs Foster impacted my childhood. She was the lady across the road from our family home who stepped in to care for my brother and I when my parents were hard pressed. My earliest memories are of her visits to our household, of her taking us in hand, and of a quality about her that still impresses itself on my memory and imagination. She exuded goodness and that fascinated me. I remember she called me a dreamer and my dreams took flight from things that fascinated me including whatever it was about Mrs Foster. It was not as if my parents lacked goodness, just that the visitor from across the road brought a freshness into the household and its quality was goodness.

I still remember the warmth of her smile. Through it her face became a pointer beyond herself to something more enduring. Allied as it was to her practical help offered to us seemingly at the drop of a hat Mrs Foster pointed to a reason and purpose to things beyond herself. Her self-forgetfulness was my first spiritual teacher since that of my parents was too much taken for granted. Her visits underlined goodness to me in such a way that I couldn't see it as other than as a gift much to be desired. When she smiled down at me in my mishaps I felt uplifted. Facing her to own up to wrongdoing seared my soul because I was made aware of my own lack of goodness.

People don't get on in the world without people to look up to and, with my parents, Mrs Foster was such a lady. As I reflect on her I judge her goodness to have been a pointer beyond herself to the world beyond this world we call heaven. Some things about life have that quality about them. In my dreams I imagine heaven as a place thrilling with the goodness of God so evident in the neighbour who went out of her way for me as a child. Indeed the act of imagining such a place is a pointer to its existence because it would be strange to imagine it unless the aspiration had been sown in my heart.

Reason and revelation

'God has set eternity in our hearts' we read in Ecclesiastes 3:11 (NIV). Again and again the words of scripture confirm our natural aspirations. The things of heaven are revealed, especially in Jesus Christ, but they are not unfamiliar to us as human beings. Are goodness, truth and beauty just there? Or do they point beyond themselves to perfect goodness, truth and beauty beyond this world? Are they part of an invitation to know, love and serve the all-loving invisible God whose love will never let go of anyone who turns to him?

Mother Teresa of Calcutta lived in the last century. She worked with great effect to care for abandoned people near to death on the streets of Calcutta. She was nicknamed a living saint and appeared quite often on UK television initially through journalist Malcolm Muggeridge who brought her work to public attention (1). Even through the media of television you sensed an extraordinary goodness about this elderly lady. I saw her smile as pointer to an indestructible goodness beyond this world. When I got to university to study Chemistry in the 1970s I had many discussions with my fellow scientists about the truth of a purely materialistic worldview. Again and again Mother Teresa would come up in conversation. I found it hard to imagine a life like hers lived to no ultimate purpose save appearing on earth then disappearing into the grave. Her life seemed to be such an excellent fruit of humanity it deserved some sort of gathering beyond this world. Her goodness seemed a remarkable pointer to heaven where I could imagine, unlike my materialist friends, a fulfilment of earthly life shed of human inadequacy.

Years later I read 'Come Be My Light' by Mother Teresa in which the saint writes of the obscuring of her faith (2). It equipped me to witness heaven to an agnostic gentleman, like me a writer, languishing in hospital with a brain tumour. I was visiting his ward when he engaged me in a conversation which touched on his envy of someone like myself who seemingly could not entertain doubt about heaven. Having listened carefully I said I was not without questions and I'd just read about Mother Teresa's questioning. As I talked a doctor striding through the ward stopped abruptly and turned to us. 'Did I hear you mention Mother Teresa? I trained with her. She gave me this medallion.' He bent down, unbuttoned his shirt and pulled out a holy medal. I was astonished and instinctively touched it, as did my agnostic friend. It was as if the saint was good enough to reach down from heaven to kindle faith in an unbeliever through an extraordinary coincidence.

As a scientist I am well trained in questioning. It's the way we get to truth. Even questioning the existence of heaven can make you open to its truth as I believe to be the case in my story of the questioning writer. Reason points us to heaven through the phenomenon of goodness which has something 'other' about it which we find difficult to accommodate to a materialist worldview. As scientific measurements get placed on graphs so scientists can extrapolate measurements and predict the future, so experience of goodness throughout our lives points us towards a goodness beyond but not against reason in that place we call heaven, 'to the spirits of the righteous made perfect' (Hebrews 12:23)

Christian belief in heaven isn't something cerebral, contrary to those thinking you build belief or disbelief by argument. In this book we present reasonable pointers to heaven but we cannot avoid the challenge heaven's existence presents which goes beyond reason. Christianity isn't a business of thinking your way into a new way of living but living your way into a new way of thinking. Over my life I have met a number of people who admit the belief in the existence of an after-life is reasonable but who fail to prioritise such belief so as to illuminate worldly concerns. Christians believe in the resurrection not with our minds but with our whole lives in response to a revelation of God helping us live out the death of the old self so the Holy Spirit can bring us new life through the agency of faith. We believe in the Cross as we make sense of suffering with the assurance that not all that happens is determined by God's plan but that all that happens is encompassed by his love. We are loved by almighty love and we are loved for ever, that is the revelation Christian faith sees for sure.

When I look ahead I'm aware of three things that will matter most: love of God, neighbour and self. It's reasonable to work on all three as best I can because I expect to have to live forever with all three commitments in heaven. It's also obedient to Christian revelation to do the same, taking to heart its talk of hell, the peril of withdrawing from love of God and neighbour. This unthinkable reality is a reduction of the three loves to one, love of self alone. I throw myself on God's mercy as I ponder this, and commend to him those who fail to know, love or serve God. They have much goodness about them and it's a puzzle to me that they do not attribute it to God though on occasion I understand their impatience with so-called godly people who fall short. Knowing I myself fall short and believing the people round me with short-comings are sent to make me good, better and fit for heaven is a challenge I couldn't face without knowing Jesus.

The goodness of Jesus

When we read the Bible we build for ourselves a picture of the unique figure of Jesus Christ. It would be totally impossible to invent a character like Jesus! The Gospels present a figure at times severe, at times compassionate, ready to give his total attention to one needy person, declaiming religious hypocrisy, upholding age old moral teaching. Jesus saw the heart of human problems as lying in the human heart and his own heart became the remedy. The endings of the Gospels and the remaining New Testament documents evidence the piercing, breaking of that heart as a revelation of the purpose of existence.

'When the goodness and loving kindness of God our Saviour appeared, he saved us, not because of any works of righteousness that we had done, but according to his mercy, through the water of rebirth and renewal by the Holy Spirit. This Spirit he poured out on us richly through Jesus Christ our Saviour, so that, having been justified by his grace, we might become heirs according to the hope of eternal life.' (Titus 3:4-7)

These words capture the centrality of the goodness of Jesus to earth and heaven. In them is stated God's saving purpose in sending his Son to populate heaven, that 'we might become heirs according to the hope of eternal life'. How? Through being made fit for friendship with God (justified) not through our own works but 'according to his mercy' shown in his Son's death, resurrection and the gift of the Spirit 'poured out on us richly through Jesus Christ our Saviour'. The goodness of Jesus is all embracing as we read in the Gospels, reaching out to include the excluded, lepers, despised tax collectors, prostitutes, thieves and most especially those outside his own native Jewish community. His passion for inclusion is rightly represented in this-worldly terms but not to the exclusion of its distinctive linked to his death and resurrection which is an invitation to inclusion of all humanity in the eternal vision at the heart of heaven.

'God our Saviour desires everyone to be saved and to come to the knowledge of the truth. For there is one God; there is also one mediator between God and humankind, Christ Jesus, himself human, who gave himself a ransom for all.' (1 Timothy 2:3b-6)

The good heart of Jesus yearns for our company in this world, through faith, and in the next world face to face, and such association the Bible calls salvation. Why is it mediated? Because perfect goodness requires it. Though the good God made humans for friendship with himself, sin breaks that friendship. The re-establishing of friendship required God to act through 'Christ Jesus, himself human, who gave himself a ransom for all' and requires us to respond to overcome sin's grip which subtracts from goodness. The dying and rising of Jesus calls forth our response 'to his mercy, through the water of rebirth and renewal by the Holy Spirit' which fits us for heaven.

'There was no other good enough to pay the price of sin. He only could unlock the gate of heaven and let us in' (3) As I reflect on Mrs Alexander's words any struggle I have with them comes back to lack of confidence in God or humility. If I argue with why Jesus Christ had to die for me I am arguing against my value to God and also against my need of that saving action, as if I were good enough for God who is perfectly good to accommodate, to shrug off lightly my bad actions and attitudes which must affront perfect goodness.

Seeking goodness

Melvyn Bragg once asked Rowan Williams what God meant to him. Here's the answer he gave: 'God is first and foremost that depth around all things and beyond all things into which, when I pray, I try to sink. But God is also the activity that comes to me out of that depth, tells me I'm loved, that opens up a future for me, that offers transformation I can't imagine. Very much a mystery but also very much a presence. Very much a person'. (4)

Seeking the goodness that fits us for heaven is a business of committing trustfully to the eternal God as the depth beyond all things, to see the world as no longer a flat surface but to descend to the goodness at the heart of all things and be impacted. To be caught up into something utterly mysterious and countercultural which is the reality of heaven. Saying our prayers, coming to Church, reading our Bibles, serving our neighbour and reflecting upon our need for God are expressions of that quest.

We seek perfect goodness as Williams describes it by relinquishing ourselves to 'that depth around all things and beyond all things into which, when (we) pray, (we) try to sink'. Such an image captures how the quest for heaven, for God, is a gracious response to God's quest for us as 'the activity that comes to (us) out of the depth, tells (us we're) loved, that opens up a future for (us)' that includes heaven. Just as floating on water is achieved by our will overcoming natural inhibition and the capacity of water to support a human body, so salvation is a business of abandoning ourselves to God.

'Sirs, what must I do to be saved?' The Philippian jailer asked Paul and Silas. 'They answered, "Believe on the Lord Jesus, and you will be saved"' (Acts 16:30:31)

Seeking goodness is seeking salvation, seeking Jesus in his perfect goodness. That quest is balanced by what we call the Gospel, the good news that God came and comes to seek us in Jesus. The best pointer to heaven is the One who came from his Father's company there with this invitation:

'Come to me, all you that are weary and are carrying heavy burdens, and I will give you rest. Take my yoke upon you, and learn from me; for I am gentle and humble in heart, and you will find rest for your souls. For my yoke is easy, and my burden is light." (Matthew 11:28-30)

Could there be a more enticing invitation? To a society stressed out by workplace achievement pressure alongside the stress of choosing between the multitude of recreational options? To relationships distorted by such stresses and difficulties agreeing such choices?

The goodness of Jesus invites our perfection but, as this invitation makes clear, he speaks to us and acts in our lives to build goodness not by imposing an impossible standard to strive for so much as accommodating our brokenness and vulnerability. Ironically it's when we admit our need, 'that we are weary carrying heavy burdens' and embrace Jesus in repentance and faith that we enter into that 'rest for our souls' which is salvation. That restful state links to the knowledge and love of God which enables us to share our lives with him in anticipation of that ultimate joyous sharing the Apostles' Creed affirms in its last paragraph: 'The communion of saints, the forgiveness of sins, the resurrection of the body and the life everlasting'. (5)

Pointers to heaven like the goodness of Mrs Foster have a ripple effect so that thanks to her, many other good people saints and my own crucial opening up to the Holy Spirit I am writing a book to be exactly such a pointer. As I do so I recall Christ's teaching in Luke 14:11 that 'all who exalt themselves will be humbled, and those who humble themselves will be exalted.` Words of Thomas More haunt me: 'whoever bids others to do right, but gives an evil example by acting the opposite way is like a foolish weaver who weaves with one hand and unravels the cloth just as quickly with the other' (6). Writing large about heaven would be presumptuous unless my own heart were set in that direction.

Goodness as a moral quality builds through life experience but it can also diminish depending on where your heart is set. It is my conviction that the vision of God is transformative of my life and its fullness will be at the heart of heaven as St John writes:

'Beloved, we are God's children now; what we will be has not yet been revealed. What we do know is this: when he is revealed, we will be like him, for we will see him as he is. And all who have this hope in him purify themselves, just as he is pure.' (1 John 3:2-3)

Seeking goodness for Christians is inseparable from seeking the vision of God and the purification necessary for that. It is also inseparable from seeking truth, subject the next Chapter, and from the truth that seeks us in Jesus Christ.

POINTERS TO HEAVEN - 2 TRUTH

Mind coming before matter points to the source of truth

I grew up fascinated by Chemistry. So much so that to the alarm of my parents I used to do experiments in the shed producing bad smells and the odd brown cloud! To discover elements first hand, like chlorine and iodine, had its dangers but growing awareness of how materials are chemically structured built my enthusiasm for science. Eventually I packed off to University and ended up researching the forces between the molecular chains in poly-thene and Teflon through neutron scattering spectroscopy. My work became part of a generation of research contributing to the emergence of light weight materials that can conduct electricity at room temperature, the components of today's phones and tab-lets. (7)

It was a pursuit of truth in which new horizons kept opening up. You felt drawn forward, motivated by something of an unveiling. What I helped discover was already there to be found. It was a matter of getting to the right place through the right theory and experimental work that confirmed the unveiling of those inter-molecular force fields. As I use my smartphone a generation on I take pleasure in knowing my research and doctorate contributed with others to the materials and design of the circuit board serv-ing its function. It's as if my seeking of the truth of things has come back to bless me.

Humans apply their minds to matter and patterns emerge. This is my first hand experience and it's been a humbling one. Discovering the patterns has naturally brought me to think about where those patterns came from. Some of my contemporaries became very famous through their study of the structure of another polymer, Deoxyribonucleic acid known as DNA. This molecule consists of two chains coiled around one other forming a double helix which carries genetic instructions for the function, growth and reproduction of all known organisms. Recent research has established what's called the 'Human Genome' or genetic code, a pattern of three billion letters that's required to create a human being.

Blessings are being reaped from this research also but there's some narrow thinking around along the lines humans are now abreast where we came from. Are we? What human being, unassisted by a computer, can oversee and think through a construction of three billion components? Yet someone, I dare to say, has done because the alternative of thousands of random actions of lesser beings is unconvincing. The truth scientists unveil, the patterns of material in a phone or a human being, is attained through a working assumption that the material world is constructed reasonably however full of surprises it is to us.

Scratch marks on a cave wall are accepted as pointing to the human intelligence of the ancients. Faced with the 3 billion components of the human genome, why are people blind to such obvious evidence for divine intelligence? If we accept Mind before matter the existence of a realm beyond the material world known to that Mind and revealed to us by him cannot be dismissed.

Reason and revelation

Just as goodness can be seen to point beyond itself perfect goodness so truth we discover in this world points to a fuller picture beyond the earth. Following such pointers, or challenging their logic, has been the occupation of philosophers down through the ages. Plato (428-348BC) is the most famous patron of a pursuit of truth running from earth into the heavens. Platonic theory is optimistic about reason's capacity to arrive unaided at the fullness of truth. Christianity rejoices at Truth's quest for us which illuminates our own quest for truth.

I am sure of heaven both because my quest for scientific truth opened up horizons that no way exclude its reality and because God in Christ reveals it. More than that, my pursuit of scientific truth led to an incident that became my teacher. I'd just celebrated my 21st birthday and was travelling on my Lambretta from Harwell, where I'd completed some neutron scattering on a polymer specimen, to Oxford. As I drove along the front tyre blew and despite repeated application of front and rear brakes the vehicle veered across the road into the path of a lorry. I said what I thought were my last prayers. Amazingly I passed just in front of the lorry landing on the kerb with a sprain to my thumb and shoulder and lived to tell the tale. Coming so close to death made for a fuller evaluation of the significance of my life. It contributed no doubt to a radical career switch a few years later from polymer scientist to parish priest.

My interrupted journey - it entailed a brief visit to hospital - pointed me beyond my own pursuit of truth to Truth's pursuit of me. Heaven came close. It became more real to me, especially as the accident occurred on 29th September, Feast of St Michael and All Angels. As for many, God became real to me not through thinking or feeling but through circumstances that stopped me literally in my tracks. It was natural to interpret my survival to divine intervention through an angel steering my scooter a shade. I lived on, and continue to live on, aware of an unseen realm and how it pierces through on occasion into our life experience.

Some time after my accident I met up with now famous priest and physicist John Polkinghorne who gave me helpful guidance. Polkinghorne in more recent years has written with clarity about how a scientific approach to truth can be harmonised with belief in God and heaven. How can science prove or disprove someone or something that's outside the observable? If you could observe God you'd be above his level and he'd no longer be God. To hold that what can be observed with your eyes or scientific instruments is all that matters is to rule out the spiritual side of things altogether. A materialistic worldview like this has moral consequences. When you set your heart on obtaining material goods you end up depriving other people of their basic needs. A narrow scientific viewpoint like materialism is good for describing what's around us. It's not good at helping us use the things around us to the best advantage. Science tells us how the world works whilst the God thing is about how it should work! In a recent book John Polkinghorne comments on how the revelation of scientific truth depends on the imagination of scientists as well as the truth awaiting revelation. The study of God, he says, similarly doesn't just depend on the seeker's imagination but also on historical facts, like those about Jesus. (8)

The truth of Jesus

Of all pointers to heaven Jesus Christ is unique on account of Christian belief in him as truly God and truly human. This belief is built on historical evidence which points to his resurrection, itself a key pointer which will be addressed later in the book. There is a human body in heaven, according to Christian revelation, that of Jesus, who awaits the company of the saints in both soul and body on his return when the dead are to be raised for his judgement. That one who still bears human flesh is appointed universal judge of who enters heaven is one of the most heartening features of 'the truth that is in Jesus' (Ephesians 4:21) as expressed in the following paragraph from the second chapter of the letter to the Hebrews.

'Jesus, who for a little while was made lower than the angels, is now crowned with glory and honour because of the suffering of death, so that by the grace of God he might taste death for everyone. It was fitting that God, for whom and through whom all things exist, in bringing many children to glory, should make the pioneer of their salvation perfect through sufferings. For the one who sanctifies and those who are sanctified all have one Father. For this reason Jesus is not ashamed to call them brothers and sisters, saying, "I will proclaim your name to my brothers and sisters, in the midst of the congregation I will praise you." And again, "I will put my trust in him." And again, "Here am I and the children whom God has given me." Since, therefore, the children share flesh and blood, he himself likewise shared the same things, so that through death he might destroy the one who has the power of death, that is, the devil, and free those who all their lives were held in slavery by the fear of death. For it is clear that he did not come to help angels, but the descendants of Abraham. Therefore he had to become like his brothers and sisters in every respect, so that he might be a merciful and faithful high priest in the service of God, to make a sacrifice of atonement for the sins of the people. (Hebrews 2:9-17)

Christians see the subject of this passage, Jesus, as the second person of the Blessed Trinity, the Son of God, who took flesh of Mary to be born Jesus the anointed one or Christ. God then is in Jesus 'tasting death for everyone' with the aim of populating the realm beyond death we call heaven, 'bringing many children to glory' making his Son 'the pioneer of their salvation'. The truth of Jesus is the truth of a holy God making himself one with his human creatures, out of love providing a remedy for sin and death by the gift of himself. God in Jesus 'had to become like his brothers and sisters in every respect, so that he might be a merciful and faithful high priest... to make a sacrifice of atonement for the sins of the people'.

The writer of this passage gave comfort to Christians under heavy persecution just 50 years or so after Jesus died and rose. Encounter with the risen Lord had built conviction of God's decisive action destroying death but the writer unpacks as fully as any New Testament writer the meaning of Christ's death as a sacrifice for sin. This is geared to bring assurance to suffering believers that God in the humanity of Jesus is not aloof from suffering, indeed expects nothing of them that he has not borne himself. The atonement spoken of is a once for all event on Calvary but it affects those in every age, not least when they are suffering. As Hebrews expresses the truth about Jesus later on: 'In the days of his flesh, Jesus offered up prayers and supplications, with loud cries and tears, to the one who was able to save him from death, and he was heard because of his reverent submission.... he became the source of eternal salvation for all who obey him (Hebrews 3:7, 9b)

Seeking truth

I have written about how my scientific career gave way to one as a priest. One of the crosses I bear is the perception to this day of some friends that my mind went soft in the process. I dare to suggest otherwise! Many a time as a Christian teacher I fall back on enquiry processes that became familiar to me through Chemistry.

I was investigating the forces between the chains in polythene and Teflon which hold clues about preparing room temperature electrical conductors such as now found in microchips. Most of the early theoretical calculations had been made in Japan. My brief in our research team was to test the Japanese force field calculations by experimentation. The experiments involved visits to the nuclear reactors at Harwell to send neutrons through carefully prepared polymer specimens. I worked out how much the neutrons accelerated as they bounced off the lattice of molecular chains. This in turn revealed something about the strength of attraction between the chains. Through systematic experimentation we were able to confirm the best force field theories from quite a wide selection.

By analogy seekers after ultimate truth are faced with many rival theories to test. The varieties of worldview are a major source of confusion to seekers after truth in our generation. Never in the history of the world have people been as aware of the rival claims of religion. Modern communications and the unprecedented flow of people have increased awareness of these alternative views making for both confusion and the opportunity to test them out. How do the different truth claims weigh up experimentally? At one level you can only answer that question by throwing yourself into allegiance to each one after the other to discover which is right. Next best we can evaluate the rival claims of faith systems according to what we perceive of their experience of the divine and their historical basis.

When I talk to adherents of Islam I applaud their sense of divine transcendence - God different to us and of heaven beyond this world. By contrast Hindu friends gain my sympathy as they talk more of divine immanence - God the same as us with allied concern for holiness of life. This comforts me as a Christian holding to God as both same and different, immanent and transcendent, centring on God's revelation in Jesus as both divine and human. Rationally I applaud the key balance maintained here which places Christianity somewhat central in the array of world religions.

Second to experience of God in various religions, historical examination of the counter claims of religion, in my opinion, favour Christianity. Though we are bound to seek truth amidst the claims and counterclaims of rival worldviews, mainstream religions claim the truth of God seeks us and leaves its mark on history. Openly agnostic about the historical basis of divine revelation Hinduism, most ancient of faiths, has spiritual wisdom formulated in myth, that is, stories containing truth for living. Islam's historical basis overlaps that of Christianity but there is as yet strong deterrence in that faith of any historical evaluation of the Quran. By contrast three centuries of critical scholarship have done little to unseat the historicity of the New Testament which centres on the event of Christ's resurrection, to be further considered in Chapter..., which is key to the Christian under-standing of God and heaven.

As I seek truth - and continue my quest with Christian allegiance - I find myself saying not 'yes, but' so much as 'yes, and' to what other faiths have to say about heaven. I say 'yes' to Islam in its affirmation of a God above and a heaven above whilst holding to his coming so close to us in Jesus that Scripture says heaven is come to earth. 'This is eternal life, that (we) may know the only true God, and Jesus Christ whom (he) has sent' (John 17:3). I say 'yes' to Hinduism in the encouragement of spiritual purification expressed in the doctrine of reincarnation but, with a rational challenge to that doctrine, hold to heaven as a gift of God in Jesus Christ to humble seekers as much as a reward for spiritual ath-letes. (9)

Scientific endeavour is in harmony with Christian discipleship inasmuch as both look to unfolding horizons, one in this world, the other in the next. In pursuing the makeup of polymers I saw an opening up of frontiers which made me feel excitement both that there was was so much unveiled before me and that this was foretaste of greater wonders awaiting discovery. All this, was my thought, and yet more to come! The microchip revolution I helped towards, with its blessings and challenges, kindles the same excitement and optimism about science's opening up of fu-ture horizons. Similarly Christian faith is a proactive quest for the ultimate unveiling of truth in heaven which is prophesied by St John the Divine in the book of Revelation.

'Then I saw a new heaven and a new earth; for the first heaven and the first earth had passed away, and the sea was no more. And I saw the holy city, the new Jerusalem, coming down out of heaven from God, prepared as a bride adorned for her husband. And I heard a loud voice from the throne saying, "See, the home of God is among mortals. He will dwell with them; they will be his peoples, and God himself will be with them; he will wipe every tear from their eyes. Death will be no more; mourning and crying and pain will be no more, for the first things have passed away." And the one who was seated on the throne said, "See, I am making all things new." Also he said, "Write this, for these words are trustworthy and true." Then he said to me, "It is done! I am the Alpha and the Omega, the beginning and the end. To the thirsty I will give water as a gift from the spring of the water of life. Those who conquer will inherit these things, and I will be their God and they will be my children. (Revelation 21:1-7)

POINTERS TO HEAVEN - 3 BEAUTY

Awesome, intriguing sights that point beyond themselves

It's hard to put into words the way music touches the spirit because what's happening is beyond words, beyond rational explanation. In my youth I discovered Beethoven and to this day I seek the tonic he provides to the spirit especially, in my own experience, through the Vivace of his seventh symphony with its dancing rhythm which lifts the heart. Beauty is in the eye or heart of the beholder but I have never doubted that it has some objective form outside of myself. Classical music through its proven popularity is a witness to how some music so grows in popularity that it gets played down through the ages. In my lifetime the melodic music of the Beatles which I play on my guitar has been seen to have power in itself. This was made evident to me on a recent visit to the cinema to watch Yesterday (10). The fictional story of singer-songwriter Jack Malik with his dreams of fame is presented. He has a freak accident during a global blackout waking into a world for whom The Beatles never existed. With all their songs in his repertoire he is gifted to play Beatles' songs to those unfamiliar with them and becomes an overnight sensation on that account. We enjoyed the film mainly because the drama was punctuated by great renditions of familiar Beatles' songs.

Goodness, truth and beauty are pointers beyond themselves and many who like myself are touched by music recognise a force beyond it which has an ultimate feel about it. One of the most popular pieces of classical music was written by the composer

Allegri in the 17th century for the Sistine Chapel in Rome. It's a setting of the penitential Psalm 51 known for short as Miserere sung repeatedly in Holy Week. The setting is for two alternating choirs one of which sings plainchant and the other a haunting chant which ascends to such a pitch it shakes the soul. The fame of the chant was increased by a Vatican prohibition on transcribing the music. In 1770 Mozart attended Holy Week services in the Chapel and wrote the chant down from memory, the origin of its popularisation that extends today to radio where it tops polls as a piece of music. Each year I try to follow Choral Evensong on Ash Wednesday broadcast by the BBC which starts with this haunting setting of Psalm 51. As I listen, following the text of the Psalm, I capture in the music a cry of lament that is is also one of ascent to God, a fearless reaching up from the depths of sin to the heights of God for his Holy Spirit. The music has the power to reach right through me drawing my attention outside of myself to a power and beauty I would call divine.

What must the one be like who breathed inspiration into Allegri so as to compose his beautiful Miserere? Or Beethoven his symphonies? Or The Beatles their melodies? I have talked to or listened to a good number of atheists over my years and I recall among them a love of music and both appreciation and bewilderment concerning its power and beauty. Beauty is a pointer we can follow beyond this world if we choose to but nothing compels us so to choose. It is intriguing, drawing us from self preoccupation into self forgetful awe.

Reason and revelation

Words crack in describing beauty. In this book I write of beauty as pointer to ultimate beauty but writing by definition lacks the dimensions that can capture the pointer. Experiencing beauty is like being struck physically so as to enter a more profound dimension of human awareness than the cerebral or emotional. Like being in a conversation which is then interrupted by something happening so the participants look away from their engagement to the cause of distraction. The experience of beauty is overwhelming and puts you in your place. Your current thoughts and feelings fade as you recognise the privilege of *just being there* before what's caught your attention. It is like the days you open the curtains and catch in one moment the rising of the sun. Your routine of life pauses, aware of something bigger and brighter than dull routine revealed to you in that moment. 'Oh come and see the dawn' might be your cry if there is someone at hand who can be invited to see the beauty. The sight of the rising sun is such a pointer it makes you a pointer to it and to what it represents.

Working in the interior of Guyana made me especially aware of the anticipation of dawn by bird song and creatures moving to position themselves to capture the warmth of the sun after overnight cool. In the same way our appreciation of beauty is increased when perceived at hard times in our life. The sight of beauty opens a window into our inner darkness or the darkness of the world we often inhabit through which glory streams in anticipation of heaven. Scriptural images of heaven have a beauty framed in description of hardship ended, as in St John the Divine's description in Revelation 7:11-17:

'After this I looked, and there was a great multitude that no one could count, from every nation, from all tribes and peoples and languages, standing before the throne and before the Lamb, robed in white, with palm branches in their hands. They cried out in a loud voice, saying, "Salvation belongs to our God who is seated on the throne, and to the Lamb!" And all the angels stood around the throne and around the elders and the four living creatures, and they fell on their faces before the throne and worshipped God, singing, "Amen! Blessing and glory and wisdom and thanksgiving and honor and power and might be to our God forever and ever! Amen." Then one of the elders addressed me, saying, "Who are these, robed in white, and where have they come from?" I said to him, "Sir, you are the one that knows." Then he said to me, "These are they who have come out of the great ordeal; they have washed their robes and made them white in the blood of the Lamb. For this reason they are before the throne of God, and worship him day and night within his temple, and the one who is seated on the throne will shelter them. They will hunger no more, and thirst no more; the sun will not strike them, nor any scorching heat; for the Lamb at the centre of the throne will be their shepherd, and he will guide them to springs of the water of life, and God will wipe away every tear from their eyes.'"

The Bible ends with this beautiful word picture. The book of Revelation like Genesis, the first book of the Bible, describes beauty rising out of chaos. By reason we can understand how human endeavour creates beauty from raw earthly material as in pots fired from clay. By revelation we are invited to see a fuller perspective of the creation of beauty out of the chaos which is in and among us as human beings. As Anthony Bloom wrote: 'We must have faith in the chaos, pregnant with beauty and harmony. We must look at ourselves as an artist looks, with vision and sobriety, at the raw material which God has put into his hands and out of which he will make a work of art' (11) Bloom's optimism about the human condition is rooted in Eastern Orthodoxy's faith in humanity as capable of becoming like God destined, as scripture states, to become 'participants in the divine nature' (2 Peter 1:4b) The beauty of the cosmos is to be surpassed by the beautiful outcome of our collaboration with God who, seeing that future and not our present chaos, can assist this growth into beauty.

When I see beautiful things or hear beautiful music it excites both my mind and my spirit. With my mind I can reason along the lines 'if these things are so, they are so different to what's routine in life I cannot explain them in rational terms other than as pointers beyond this world'. It is reasonable to see something 'other' in the experience of beauty. With my spirit, though, I can directly engage with the 'otherness' of beauty, touched by the gift of the Holy Spirit who opens up convincingly the beauty of what is revealed of heaven in Revelation 7. As Paul teaches in 1 Corinthians 2:9b-13:

'What no eye has seen, nor ear heard, nor the human heart conceived, what God has prepared for those who love him" - these
things God has revealed to us through the Spirit; for the Spirit
searches everything, even the depths of God. For what human
being knows what is truly human except the human spirit that
is within? So also no one comprehends what is truly God's except the Spirit of God. Now we have received not the spirit of the
world, but the Spirit that is from God, so that we may understand
the gifts bestowed on us by God. And we speak of these things in
words not taught by human wisdom but taught by the Spirit, in-
terpreting spiritual things to those who are spiritual.'

The beauty of Jesus

Janet was Churchwarden in my first parish. Through her deep faith
and loving support for many she was a key instrument in building
up the church over the time I served as parish priest. We were all
shocked by the speed of her decline with a terminal illness. It was
my privilege to take Holy Communion to her day by day as she
approached death. In this rite the consecrated bread is taken to
the home from the Eucharist in Church. Janet's devotion to Jesus
was such that the two of us would spend some minutes preparing
for Communion by gazing in anticipation at the holy bread before
she received it. Through that day by day practice over her last
month on earth I became aware of her loving gaze of anticipation
before the Lord came to her in Communion. I shall never forget
it and associate it with a song we used to sing then in Church:
'Turn your eyes upon Jesus, look full in his wonderful face, and
the things of earth will grow strangely dim in the light of his glory
and grace'.

I believe Janet is in heaven. I cannot believe her yearning gaze
upon the beauty of Jesus veiled in the Sacrament is not fulfilled
with the unveiled vision of God, that such evident desire for the
Lord in this world has not melted into union with him in heaven.

Among all the beautiful things in the world Jesus Christ is paramount because of the beauty which shines from him alone in the darkest of places, the death bed. Looking back on the experience of bringing Communion to Janet, struck down in untimely fashion, I recall the day by day consolation her devotion gave me, as well as her family, as she looked to the Lord. It influenced me to make Psalm 34:5 our church motto for a time: 'Look to the Lord and be radiant' (Jerusalem Bible).

The beauty we see on earth is a pointer to the perfect beauty of heaven but the link is not straightforward, as we shall consider later in the chapter on suffering. When we follow the account of the earthly life of Jesus we see moral and spiritual beauty. That beauty is subservient to the immense beauty revealed in his death and resurrection since, as at Janet's deathbed, the beauty of Jesus shines clearest when we turn to him in our darkness.
One incident in the account of his earthly life of Jesus anticipates this full beauty of even before his resurrection.

'Jesus took with him Peter and John and James, and went up on the mountain to pray. And while he was praying, the appearance of his face changed, and his clothes became dazzling white. Suddenly they saw two men, Moses and Elijah, talking to him. They appeared in glory and were speaking of his departure, which he was about to accomplish at Jerusalem. Now Peter and his companions were weighed down with sleep; but since they had stayed awake, they saw his glory and the two men who stood with him. Just as they were leaving him, Peter said to Jesus, "Master, it is good for us to be here; let us make three dwellings, one for you, one for Moses, and one for Elijah"—not knowing what he said. While he was saying this, a cloud came and overshadowed them; and they were terrified as they entered the cloud. Then from the cloud came a voice that said, "This is my Son, my Chosen; listen to him!"' (Luke 9:28b-35)

What is extraordinary about Christianity compared to other revealed religions is its historical base. The story of Jesus is widely accepted by scholars as possessing a strong historical foundation. Even the resurrection is not discounted as such by many. Three of the four Gospel accounts place the incident of the transfiguration of Jesus, as here in Luke, central to their account of his ministry as a pivotal moment. The mountain setting underlines Jesus as connecting earth and heaven as does the dazzling beauty he manifests. The voice of God and the presence of Moses and Elijah reinforce his uniqueness as one to 'listen to'. Jesus had taught God is 'God not of the dead but of the living' (Matthew 22:32) which is demonstrated through long dead Moses and Elijah appearing with him in God's presence opening up a vision of heaven as dwelling place of those who face death with faith in him. Death, like the dark cloud terrifying the apostles in the account, is subject to the risen Lord Jesus who waits to reveal his beauty in the darkness as was our experience at Janet's passing.

Seeking beauty

'In Dostoevsky's The Idiot, Prince Myskin sees a painting by Hans Holbein the Younger depicting Christ dead in the tomb and says: "Looking at that painting might cause one to lose his faith." The painting is a gruesome portrayal of the destructive effects of death on Christ's body. Yet it is precisely in contemplating Jesus' death that faith grows stronger and receives a dazzling light; then it is revealed as faith in Christ's steadfast love for us, a love capable of embracing death to bring us salvation. This love, which did not recoil before death in order to show its depth, is something I can believe in; Christ's total self-gift overcomes every suspicion and enables me to entrust myself to him completely' (12) In those words Pope Francis demonstrates a paradox in our seeking beauty. He quotes from Dostoevsky's Idiot in which the hero, Christ-figure Prince Myskin, displays a strange beauty against the back cloth of drunkards, liars and murderers who are intrigued by his selflessness (13). It is in this work that Dostoevsky utters his most famous quotation: 'beauty will save the world' which is developed in the Pope's reflection in his encyclical *Lumen Fidei.* The beauty of Holbein's gruesome Christ is opened up by faith which sees in it 'Christ's total self-gift (which) overcomes every suspicion and enables me to entrust myself to him completely'.

In an age where you have to double check what you read for fear of untruth, in which goodness is seen so little in the public domain we are wise to continue to seek beauty through music and the arts in the hope it will point us heavenwards. Not that music and art are incapable of deception for beauty is in the eye of the beholder, an eye so often clouded by spiritual cataracts. To seek beauty is to be on the road to heaven. It also brings an obligation to cleanse your spiritual vision by casting off suspicion and distrust, as the Pope suggests, besides turning away from unhelpful self-regard.

When did you last visit an art gallery or attend a music concert? Both experiences have the power to take us out of ourselves into 'beauty that will save the world' most especially sacred art and music. I recall in idle moments strolling through London's National Gallery only to be engaged with a picture painted by someone of faith that energises me, brings a wake up tonic to my own faith. In the same way attending eucharist or evensong sung in a place like St Paul's or Westminster Cathedral impacts me in a way beyond my day to day routine engagement with worship. Seeking beauty as a person of faith opens up a wider timeless dimension. The space of the Cathedral with saints and angels in mosaic over your head becomes heaven's antechamber. The alleluias of the choir anticipate heaven's triumph. As Bishop William Waltham How writes in his famous hymn for All Saints Day: 'And when the strife is fierce, the warfare long, steals on the ear the distant triumph song, and hearts are brave, again, and arms are strong. Alleluia, Alleluia!' (14)

POINTERS TO HEAVEN - 4 HOLINESS

People with something about them beyond this world

I'd been brought up as a Church-goer but it wasn't until I went to a Church with a saint as parish priest that heaven came real. It was St Mary Magdalene's in Oxford and the Vicar was John Hooper. What intrigued me at first was preaching rather different to the lectures I attended as an Oxford undergraduate. Here was a presentation less analytical and balanced and more synthetic and fervent. I found the word for it eventually - 'doxological' - addressed in praise to God. Fr John brought the Eucharist alive through his evident reverence and conviction. I began to see St Mary Mags as an outpost of heaven with its array of clergy and servers facing the altar as if towards God, incense rising heavenwards and singing from the choir which left me space to pray inwardly.

In those days there was no news sheet, parish magazine let alone website but a warm, friendly congregation unobtrusively English in their giving space to one another. The draw of the Church was such you might have to kneel in the aisle if you got there late on Sunday. I can recall no evangelism scheme, just worship day by day and priests ready for one-to-one engagement with those who were interested. On occasion Fr Hooper would invite undergraduates for afternoon tea at the Vicarage. Over a wide ranging conversation the issue of sacramental confession came up one day I came to tea. I felt something hit me inside as the priest commended it. There was something charismatic about Hooper, something beyond this world, so what he spoke about though sometimes illogical could come at you with a force from beyond him. Days later I made my first Confession. It was a turning point in my spiritual life which was from then more fully Christian, turning from sin, heading for heaven.

'Holiness is the church's greatest influence' wrote Pascal. 'People almost invariably arrive at their beliefs not on the basis of proof but on the basis of what they find attractive' (15). This is exactly my experience. In this book, I set forth reasons or pointers to heaven, not proofs, but lines that can convince seen in concert. When I arrived in Oxford I had Christianity in the sense of pieces of a jig saw that seemed to fit. It was through meeting a man of exceptional holiness that the pieces came together and I met Jesus Christ of whom Hooper was icon. Even as I write about his influence words crack again in the attempt to explain how the world to come opened up through the Eucharist and through engaging with holiness. Christianity points to heaven faithful to its Founder, Jesus Christ who rose from the dead. The Church as an outpost of heaven is seen in the supernatural quality of its members, a quality best captured in the word 'holiness'.

Reason and revelation

Among the congregation in the St Mary Mags of my day were two more hard headed priests, the future Bishop of Salisbury John Baker and the philosopher theologian Austin Farrer, both of whom Fr John would embarrass quoting them in his sermons! I owe to both writers a rational defence of heaven which has helped me consolidate inspiration to belief in the world to come revealed to me through John Hooper. All three mentors have helped convince me the only meaningful thing in life is what conquers death, not what but Who!

John Austin Baker writes: 'I rest on God, who will assuredly not allow me to find the meaning of life in his love and forgiveness, to be wholly dependent on him for the gift of myself, and then destroy that meaning, revoke that gift. He who holds me in existence now can and will hold me in it still, through and beyond the dissolution of my mortal frame. For this is the essence of love, to affirm the right of the beloved to exist. And what God affirms, nothing and no-one can contradict'. (16) In other words belief in heaven is a logical corollary of love's affirmation of the beloved and the nature of almighty love which transcends our mortality as demonstrated in the resurrection of Jesus.

Austin Farrer writes: 'I tell you Christianity cannot for any length of time survive the amputation of such a limb as life to come. For God has put his infinity in our mind, and if we cannot stretch out for him beyond the little beginnings here allowed us, we must let go of God and loose him wholly. For we can only have God if God has us; and if he will not make a job of us and bring us to union with his glorious infinity, how can we believe that he has taken hold of us at all? What is our salvation, but that we are in the hands of God? And what are the hands of God, if they are weaker than animal death?' (17) Again Farrer, like Baker, stresses the supernatural basis of Christianity and how disbelief in heaven is inconsistent with belief in God as both almighty and all-loving.

It was Fr Austin Farrer that brought the last sacraments to his friend C.S.Lewis, a third great Christian apologist with a St Mary Magdalen, Oxford connection. Though Lewis wrote in a non-partisan way so as to appeal across the Christian tradition he was familiar in the Confession queue before Festivals in the St Mary Mags of his day. His Anglocatholicism, like that of Baker, Farrer and Hooper, was a thoughtful Christianity whilst obedient to the faith of the church through the ages. The epitaph on his Westminster Abbey memorial expresses how revelation and reason are intertwined in Christian faith: 'I believe in Christianity as I believe that the Sun has risen, not only because I see it but because by it I see everything else' (18). The quotation reminds me that though we cannot see God or heaven he does give us through the inner eye of holy faith a capacity to see him, especially in Jesus Christ, and, as Lewis says, once you see God in that way you're bound to see all things in that light including life after death.

St Paul talks about the transformative light of faith in his second letter to the Corinthians: 'All of us, with unveiled faces, seeing the glory of the Lord as though reflected in a mirror, are being transformed into the same image from one degree of glory to another; for this comes from the Lord, the Spirit. Yet, the god of this world has blinded the minds of the unbelievers, to keep them from seeing the light of the gospel of the glory of Christ, who is the image of God. For we do not proclaim ourselves; we proclaim Jesus Christ as Lord and ourselves as your slaves for Jesus' sake. For it is the God who said, 'Let light shine out of darkness', who has shone in our hearts to give the light of the knowledge of the glory of God in the face of Jesus Christ'. (2 Corinthians 3:18, 4:4-6)

Such knowledge is gained by holy encounter with God and believers, a revelation supplementing the reasonable basis of Christianity in the incontestable yet provocative history of its founder.

The holiness of Jesus

The force behind John Hooper challenged my selfish preoccupation. The 'something about him' intrigued me. It led me out of my comfort zone in chemical research into another realm of engagement. The opening of Mark's Gospel has a similar dynamic of folk taken somewhat inexplicably from one occupation to another. 'As Jesus passed along the Sea of Galilee, he saw Simon and his brother Andrew casting a net into the sea - for they were fishermen. And Jesus said to them, "Follow me and I will make you fish for people." And immediately they left their nets and followed him. As he went a little farther, he saw James son of Zebedee and his brother John, who were in their boat mending the nets. Immediately he called them; and they left their father Zebedee in the boat with the hired men, and followed him.' (Mark 1:16-20)

What was so different about Jesus? It seems the sight of him, the glance of his eyes pulled folk right out of their current preoccupation into discipleship. The answer links to an incident recorded even nearer the start of Mark's Gospel when, we read, 'Jesus came from Nazareth of Galilee and was baptized by John in the Jordan. And just as he was coming up out of the water, he saw the heavens torn apart and the Spirit descending like a dove on him. And a voice came from heaven, "You are my Son, the Beloved; with you I am well pleased."' (Mark 1:9-11) Jesus conceived by the Holy Spirit lived 30 years before the Spirit manifested in power at his baptism after which an extraordinary dynamic emerged that engaged others starting with the fishermen Simon, Andrew, James and John. They were swept off their feet by something about Jesus, 'God's Son, the Beloved' and that 'something' was the Holy Spirit.

The holiness of Jesus reflects God's eternal presence entering the here and now of mortal beings. It is our supreme pointer and pull towards heaven. Those disciples were dragged from their fishing to a higher work which would involve them gathering others to faith in Christianity's founder. As we read through the Gospel accounts we pick up a note of urgency as Jesus moves with followers from place to place culminating in his suffering, death and resurrection in Jerusalem. 'Today, tomorrow, and the next day I must be on my way, because it is impossible for a prophet to be killed outside of Jerusalem.' (Luke 13:33) In Jesus we see God and we see him as similar and as different to us. Similar in his oneness with sinful humanity, different in his oneness with God in his holiness. In his holiness Jesus had sight of heaven's otherworldly glory whilst possessing unique awareness of the depth and depravity of human nature. By the power of the Holy Spirit Jesus comes to dwell in the women and men of faith forming his Church bringing them transformation into an infectious holiness that fits us for heaven.

The operation of Christ's holiness in the world through the Church resembles that of blood renewing damaged tissue in the human body. It is a hidden activity which, as with the expulsion of cancerous tissue, builds life-giving health of body, mind and spirit within harmonious relationships. Through his Holy Spirit Christ operates as life-giver when invited to counter the death-dealing forces opposed to our well being. 'If the Spirit of him who raised Jesus from the dead dwells in you, he who raised Christ from the dead will give life to your mortal bodies also through his Spirit that dwells in you.' (Romans 8:11)

The fishermen captivated by the holiness of Jesus dropped their nets and their livelihood to set off with him to engage with a task which continues to this day of fitting mortals for immortality, the disobedient for God's praise and sinners for heaven. Like the dragomen of old sent ahead in the desert to prepare a resting place for travellers Jesus in his holiness prepares the place ahead for his followers we call heaven. 'In my Father's house there are many dwelling places. If it were not so, would I have told you that I go to prepare a place for you? And if I go and prepare a place for you, I will come again and will take you to myself, so that where I am, there you may be also. And you know the way to the place where I am going... I am the way, and the truth, and the life. No one comes to the Father except through me.' (John 14:2-4, 6)

Seeking holiness

I want to reach heaven. I recognise the need to prepare for it and that recognition is a pointer to heaven's existence. In our minds we find it hard to imagine folk excluded from heaven since such exclusion looks mean spirited and inconsistent with the love of God. Something within us challenges that logic. As the great theologian Karl Barth wrote, 'we hope that all will be saved but act as though that were not so'. There is a deep instinct of aspiration opened up by encounter with holiness that runs counter to self-will. That aspiration is evidence of what it aspires to. Looking back on what opened up to me over a cup of tea with Fr Hooper, it was as if something within me previously comatose woke up and got me going spiritually. I was able to see another dimension to my life, how my moral failures were unworthy of this realm and needed addressing by repentance. There was something much bigger about life than I had ever imagined.

Throughout my life I've been grateful for occasional wake up calls like the one first provided over tea in an Oxford Vicarage. They have reminded me, yes, that God loves me but, secondly, he loves me too much to ignore failings counter to his holiness. In the New Testament we pick up a four fold pattern for deepening holiness - repent, believe, ask, receive. When something happens to show we are living wrong its a call to wake up and put things right. Repentance is an awakening, a recognition we have been in the wrong. It links to putting faith in the better future God holds before us, to asking for his help and to receiving the Holy Spirit afresh. Sharing our need for forgiveness with the Church as in the sacrament of confession recognises how our failings affect others, as the faults of a player affect the team they play in. Seeking the Holy Spirit in repentance binds us closer to the communion of saints fitting us for heaven.

Holiness disarms pride. It is an invitation to lose self-importance, recognise the importance of others and God above all. Seeking holiness is about seeking the influence of Jesus upon our lives whose closeness to God and to humanity equip him to open up the best future for us including heaven. Can we imagine a realm like this without self-love? Only when love of self is allied to love of everyone and everything, something we gain sight of from time to time especially in worship.

The vision at worship of other-worldly holiness in Chapter 6 of the Old Testament prophet Isaiah provides texts included in the Christian worship of the eucharist to this day. Isaiah' seeking of holiness became God's wake up call for service.

'In the year that King Uzziah died, I saw the Lord sitting on a throne, high and lofty; and the hem of his robe filled the temple. Seraphs were in attendance above him; each had six wings: with two they covered their faces, and with two they covered their feet, and with two they flew. And one called to another and said: "Holy, holy, holy is the Lord of hosts; the whole earth is full of his glory." The pivots on the thresholds shook at the voices of those who called, and the house filled with smoke. And I said: "Woe is me! I am lost, for I am a man of unclean lips, and I live among a people of unclean lips; yet my eyes have seen the King, the Lord of hosts!" Then one of the seraphs flew to me, holding a live coal that had been taken from the altar with a pair of tongs. The seraph touched my mouth with it and said: "Now that this has touched your lips, your guilt has departed and your sin is blotted out." Then I heard the voice of the Lord saying, "Whom shall I send, and who will go for us?" And I said, "Here am I; send me!" (Isaiah 6:1-8)

There are times in my life when I see the love of God surrounding me as like a soothing warm bath. Other times the experience of God's holiness, strikes me as like that of Isaiah, more of a cold shower, bracing me for action. Isaiah's vision of heavenly worship is awesome capturing our insignificance before God alongside his provision of the cleansing we need to be made part of it. This scripture is an awesome pointer to the invitation to eternal fellowship from a loving God whose holiness is affronted by our sin. Christians through the ages have seen Jesus as the live coal in Isaiah's vision, cleansing those who welcome him of guilt and sin, fitting them for the holiness distinctive of the world to come.

Something of what dawned on Isaiah dawned on me years ago when I first saw the rising incense at the Eucharist in St Mary Magdalene, Oxford offered by its saintly priest. Like a film preview it became for me taster of the forthcoming attraction of heaven.

POINTERS TO HEAVEN - 5 LOVE

Serving others, building justice, points to ultimate harmony

I left Oxford to train for ordination at Mirfield in my native Yorkshire where I joined the Company of Mission Priests serving in Doncaster. It's an excellent group of mission-oriented clergy working often in clergy houses in the neediest places in the UK best served by single priests. CMP clergy do not make a celibacy vow of but make an annual promise with that intention. After eight wonderful years in the Company, though, I found myself unexpectedly praying about marriage. To my bemusement God put me in touch with a member of the Company, Canon John Dorman seeking CMP support for training Amerindian priests in Guyana, South America. I accepted this as God's call, surrendering the hope of marriage, since I recognised the importance of helping provide Christian teaching and sacraments across Guyana's immense hinterland.

Preparation for this mission meant six months orientation at the United Society for the Propagation of the Gospel (USPG) College in Selly Oak. Impatient to get on with my mission it seemed an excessive demand. It proved to be a blessing above many blessings since attending College at that time brought me contact with an attractive widow, Anne with whom an 'understanding' developed! She was heading to Argentina to work for the Bishop and did so as I left for Guyana, both of us praying God would shorten our time apart. He did so through the Bishop of Argentina releasing Anne and the boys to travel north to Guyana's interior where we were married by an Amerindian priest. It worked out that Anne played a key role in the training of priests through her gift of friendship which helped build relationships between the wives of those preparing. When we see how people nowadays find their spouses through the internet we count our blessings that another external, transnational agency became our matchmaker. Anne and I 'have known and believe the love that God has for us. God is love, and those who abide in love abide in God, and God abides in them'. (1 John 4:16)

Both Anne and I had recently lost loved ones in the prime of life, her first husband, Robert, and my brother, Tony. In coming to terms with our bereavements Christian conviction that human life is preparatory for heaven was important alongside the conviction expressed in Romans that 'all things work together for good for those who love God, who are called according to his purpose' (Romans 8:28). That seemed the case with our coming together through trials that had not caused us to swerve away from loving God. The joy of coming together by his guiding hand seemed inseparable from the same hand's involvement in the suffering that led up to our meeting, something we will consider later in the book. Anne's conviction that her first husband Robert, drowned in a tragic accident, is safe with God in heaven remains a great inspiration as is her powerful written work of testimony, 'Mightier than the waves' (19).

Reason and revelation

In marriage we enter a new school of self-forgetfulness particularly when children arrive needing 24-7 care for years on end. When successful such giving and receiving of love can be a pointer to God's self gift within himself and that of the communion of saints in heaven. If human beings are made in God's image they are best pointers to God, particularly when showing God-like generosity to one another. The hospitality of believing families goes further. It is rooted in a desire to make the stranger welcome which is an expression and overflow of the love of God.

'Welcome one another, therefore, just as Christ has welcomed you, for the glory of God.' (Romans 15:7)

Our lives are frail, however old we are, and they are also full of beauty. We mortals stand like sand castles before the sea, but we contain within us the solid fabric of eternity in the love we bear to others. When the tide of death sweeps over us it will remove useless self regard and leave us with the thing that lasts – love for God and people. That can't be swept aside. It stands for ever as a component of the communion of saints. When death's tide sweeps over the sandcastle of our lives it will reveal how much heavenly substance there is within us sorting that from what is sandy and ephemeral. That solid residue will be our outgoing concern that draws us out of ourselves into generous communion with others.

The experience of love by individuals and communities is a key component of the world to come where generous communion with one another is complete. This links to the desire to see justice done with heaven seen as where that will finally be so. Yet justice in popular thinking is sometimes set against love. People see getting justice as getting judgement in a harsh unloving sense. Others see love in a weak sense, as nonjudgmental acceptance. Love and justice are closer than both these distortions so that justice can be seen as nothing less than the public face of love. This has relevance to our imagination of what heaven is like in terms of relationships. On earth we live with unjust relationships between privileged and unprivileged, educated and illiterate, rich and poor, strong and weak. In heaven there is no levelling out so much as voluntary re-balancing in love, a harnessing of the gifts of the strong into the service of all.

Vincent de Paul was ordained as a priest in 1600 aged 19. In his youth he ministered to the wealthy and powerful. The experience of pastoring prisoners made to work galley boats by rowing in confined ranks inspired him to raise up care given to this day by his Vincentian followers to the marginalised and powerless.

His advice captures the reasonable link between love and justice: 'Love the poor. Honour them, as you would honour Christ himself... Deal with their most urgent needs. Organise charity so that it is more efficient... teach reading and writing, educate with the aim of giving each the means of self-support. Intervene with authorities to obtain reforms in structure... there is no charity without justice' (20) Vincent's receiving personal revelation of God's self-giving love fuelled his care of the marginalised. This revelation allied itself to reasonable working out of such care through challenging injustices that keep the marginalised marginalised.

The passion for justice is fuelled by love in a strong sense which runs counter to powers that consciously or unconsciously make people second class in their society. It points to the levelling of all humans before the awesome reality of God and the good news of his invitation for all to share equal glory with him in heaven if they so choose.

The love of Jesus

Religion is God-given but it gets man-handled! Such 'man-handling' is obvious to many through mass media and has led to a widespread cynicism about what's at the heart of religion, the 'God-given' side. When a fanatic kills themselves and others shouting praise to God they dehumanise themselves, their victims and those who, reflecting on their act, turn away from God themselves. It's bold to say religion puts humanity in its right mind when it clearly puts some folk in their wrong mind. What keeps me defending religion - Christianity - is its central revelation of God as one with no favourites save everyone and everything revealed in Jesus Christ.

Do you know the parable of the Good Samaritan? Do you see it as an example of how to care for the needy? It is far more than that. Here it is for our examination:

'A man was going down from Jerusalem to Jericho, and fell into the hands of robbers, who stripped him, beat him, and went away, leaving him half dead. Now by chance a priest was going down that road; and when he saw him, he passed by on the other side. So likewise a Levite, when he came to the place and saw him, passed by on the other side. But a Samaritan while travelling came near him; and when he saw him, he was moved with pity. He went to him and bandaged his wounds, having poured oil and wine on them. Then he put him on his own animal, brought him to an inn, and took care of him. The next day he took out two denarii, gave them to the innkeeper, and said, "Take care of him; and when I come back, I will repay you whatever more you spend.' Which of these three, do you think, was a neighbour to the man who fell into the hands of the robbers?" [The questioner] said, "The one who showed him mercy." Jesus said to him, "Go and do likewise."' (Luke 11:30-37)

This parable is an eloquent revelation of what love is in practice. Jesus tells the story in answer to a question about what it is practically and under God to love your neighbour. To gain the force of the teaching we need to understand Jewish ritual laws concerning touching a corpse. The priest and Levite knew these laws which is most likely why they passed by. What mattered to them was keeping right with God by following his rules as they perceived them. That the man lying by the roadside might not yet be a corpse was, to our astonishment, a secondary consideration. Then someone enters the story not bound by such laws but by the wider law of humanity, the Samaritan. This Jewish outsider sees the man by the roadside and imagining his suffering, taking it to heart, is 'moved with pity' to engage with the stranger saving his life. The parable of the Good Samaritan presents God as on the side of what is most humane, a crashing criticism of wrongheaded inhumane religion. Can we imagine the fury of the priests and Levites hearing the parable? How would they see this denunciation of their religion, a religion for those paid up into it, for those following and never breaking outdated inhumane rules?

In the parable of the Good Samaritan we see the love of God taught by Jesus as extending not just over those faithful to the narrow Judaism of his day but reaching over all. It's the most radical of messages. Behind it is a view that heaven cannot be earned by rule keeping but is the gift of God to those who will welcome him. The Founder of Christianity taught religion as that which brings humanity into its right mind as exemplified by the Samaritan, himself, to Jews, a religious outsider. As we enter the depths of this parable in Luke 11 the conflict which brings Jesus to death and resurrection in Chapters 22-24 is clarified. It is summarised in the canticle Te Deum Laudamus:

'You, Christ, are the King of glory, the eternal Son of the Father.
When you took our flesh to set us free you humbly chose the Virgin's womb.
You overcame the sting of death and opened the kingdom of heaven to all believers. You are seated at God's right hand in glory.
We believe that you will come and be our judge.
Come then, Lord, and help your people, bought with the price of your own blood,
and bring us with your saints to glory everlasting'. (21)

The love of Jesus 'opens the kingdom of heaven to all believers'. It is love without partiality, the love of God for all that is, just because it is, and not because of a religious deal. Unconditional love, taught and demonstrated. At the end of Luke's Gospel one of the thieves crucified besides Christ calls out: "Jesus, remember me when you come into your kingdom." He replied, "Truly I tell you, today you will be with me in Paradise." (Luke 23:42)

Of all pointers to heaven these words of the trusting thief are most graphic. They speak of a love powerful and inclusive which anticipates that which holds the communion of saints beyond death where 'the last will be first, and the first will be last' (Matthew 20:16)

Seeking love

Giving and receiving love is wonderful, so wonderful many see it as *the* pointer to heaven. My experience of marriage to Anne and of sharing life with our children and grandchildren never seems an end in itself. Through faith, but also reasonable reflection, it is hard to see this as a mere 'sand castle' to be swept away by the 'tide' of death. Sacrificial love in and outside of families seems to head somewhere beyond this world, a quality death's tide will actually reveal. I am aware of how much selfishness there is in me, often being reminded by close interaction within my family. If 'charity begins at home' it ends in heaven. For now the challenge is to see love grow within and around us.

Seeking love is about expanding our vision of the world, of ourselves and of our destiny. In my experience the greatest challenge is my perceived self-sufficiency. Part of my up-bringing living in a prosperous culture self-sufficiency is a natural development which I am thankfully finding more and more challenged. If love makes the world - this world and the next - go round, it shakes self-sufficiency taking me out of myself towards others. Seeking love, seeking to receive love, is a profound spiritual challenge to me and to many in my acquaintance. Over many years I have been privileged to mentor some gifted and high achieving people whose incapacity to receive love has come close to being their undoing. I think of the multi-millionaire business man whose hard work took him away from seeking to receive from his wife - his was all the giving - and how their marriage dissolved. By contrast I think of Bernard, regular attender at the eucharist, whose life was turned upside down as for the first time he welcomed God's love deep in his heart by seeking the Holy Spirit. I will never forget his appearance all grins on my doorstep early one morning to tell me he had received a new gift of prayer including speaking in tongues!

Many 'church regulars' have more duty than joy about us despite being part of a 'colony of heaven' on earth. Where churches capture such love and joy from God they are seen as truly such outposts, pointers to the unalloyed joy and perfect love of heaven. A relative of mine has had learning difficulties throughout her life. She lives a long way from us and from time to time we catch up with her. Recently we spent the weekend near her and went to her Church. It was an extraordinary experience for me. The parish eucharist had a high degree of informality. The priest conducted an orchestra of contributors to the service several challenged by mental health issues. There was a warmth and inclusion in that eucharist which brought a phrase in the service alive in a new way, 'blessed are those who are called to his supper' (Revelation 19:9). The receiving and giving of love among people from all walks of life, most especially disabled pushed to the margins elsewhere, made me think of heaven. As we shall consider later, worship is a key pointer to heaven. Where worship is raised by a loving fellowship such as I experienced that Sunday, there is a sense of awe so the eucharist anticipates the fully inclusive and joy-filled supper of heaven.

How can we grow love? As the defining ingredient of heaven it needs both defining and refining in our lives. Love has many definitions ranging from selfish appetite through friendship, marriage and work for justice towards the sacrificial self-giving of martyrs. Here is where the love of Jesus Christ, and his acceptance of wherever our love lies on that spectrum, can prove transformative to those who seek God through him. In seeking and finding him we see how all that is is loved everlastingly by almighty love. Welcoming such love is no quick-fix but a constant process of pushing away pride and self-sufficiency to welcome the Holy Spirit. In my experience focussing on my sinful shortcomings can be self-defeating. Repentance concerning failures in love is best allied to seeking God's perfect love in worship, prayer, study of the bible and the lives of the saints and forming self-forgetfulness in the service of others. Another aid is spiritual direction, otherwise known as soul friendship, in which we take courage to open ourselves to a trusted fellow who can help us in the life-long journey of faith. As St Therese of Lisieux writes, the best evidence of being on this journey anticipating heaven is peace in the heart through knowing God is making us more and more an instrument of his love:

'Merit does not consist in doing or giving much, but in receiving, in loving much... Jesus wants to make his own the blessedness of giving... he does not teach me to count my acts but to do everything for love, to refuse him nothing... but all this in peace, in abandonment. Jesus does everything, I nothing.' (22)

POINTERS TO HEAVEN
- 6 SUFFERING

Seeing meaning in suffering or facing a greater question

The most chilling aspect of my brother Tony's suicide was the receipt for the gas cylinder and large plastic bag purchased two months before he used them to end his life. Though his death was swift and painless planning it for weeks in advance revealed his depth of despair. As manager of a failing theatre costume company in São Paulo, Brazil, he seems to have decided that the day he could not pay his workers would be his last. Neither my mother or I had picked up the gravity of his financial crisis in regular phone calls so when his bank manager phoned me to say he had committed suicide I could not at first believe it. It was the saddest day of my life bringing me responsibility to break the news of my brother's death to our widowed mother. I made a five hour train journey arriving at her home 10pm to bring a message in person from the night in every sense. Both of us began a period of suffering we will carry to our graves.

To lose your only sibling at 33 years takes away one who helps recall from nearest to your perspective your childhood, adolescence and early career. Like many brothers with a two year gap we were in competition. Tony was more charismatic with a wider circle of friends. He was less focussed and sat more lightly to religious adherence. As such he was a great foil, challenging and sharpening my thinking, helping me to see it's in giving out that we receive and build friendships. The suffering was like losing a limb and initially threw my life out of balance. It brought full responsibility for my ageing mother's welfare. Bereavement through suicide has such sharpness with the painful haunting question: 'if, only..'. Could I have phoned him more? Of course I could, though what difference it would have made is another question. So many of his peers, girlfriend included, were as astonished by Tony's suicide as we were.

When you suffer, self pity is natural. Our makeup means setbacks to body, mind or spirit call forth attention to self to allay the pain. I recall the patience of friends listening to me expressing grief and, yes, anger. The death of a loved one deliberately, without notice and in a fashion seemingly forgetful of those they leave behind, especially their widowed mother, is galling. Only as fuller circumstances of Tony's death emerged over the weeks that followed did I build forgiveness towards him. The clinical planning of his suicide evidenced deep isolation despite his having a business partner who could have taken more financial responsibility if he had been alerted. Anger at a bereavement such as this was and still is on occasion directed against the universe and God for allowing such a tragedy and the accompanying grief and suffering. At the same time it was and is the taking an eternal perspective to Tony's death that has eased suffering over the years besides helping me sympathise with others who have suffered the suicide of a loved one. In suffering bereavement we rediscover our humanity as John Donne captures famously:

'All mankind is of one author, and is one volume; when one man dies, one chapter is not torn out of the book, but translated into a better language; and every chapter must be so translated... As therefore the bell that rings to a sermon, calls not upon the preacher only, but upon the congregation to come: so this bell calls us all... No man is an island, entire of itself... any man's death diminishes me, because I am involved in mankind; and therefore never send to know for whom the bell tolls; it tolls for thee.' (23)

Reason and revelation

Suffering is a pointer to heaven where the eye of faith invites an eternal perspective to make sense of it. That apart it seems pointer to a cruel unintelligible world. Few writers have captured the challenge of this apparent meaningless of life better than the French philosopher Albert Camus in 'The Myth of Sisyphus'. In Greek mythology, Sisyphus pushed a boulder up a hill, saw it roll down the other side and pushed it back up again, endlessly repeating that process. Camus compares his futile search for the meaning of life in the face of suffering to the quest of Sisyphus. His conclusion is once you realise life's absurdity you are forced to make protest at this. This voiced and acted revolt is like the hard work of Sisyphus, granting contentment, as for a tasked labourer in the face of a world devoid of truth, meaning or God. A Nobel laureate, brought up in poverty, who fought for the French Resistance, charismatic and principled, Camus wrote his influential essay on Sisyphus during the bleakest period of the 1939-1945 World War. It presented a challenge to the Christian ascendancy of his day in affirming the reality of evil, its moral challenge and the need to counter the suffering of the innocent. (24)

The moral strength of Camus in describing the enormity of human suffering and the associated problem of its meaning is widely recognised. He is no cynic even though suffering breeds widespread cynicism about the reason and purpose for life. Writers like Camus show how capacity to reflect on suffering compounds it, with human suffering maybe worst in the animal kingdom on that account. The ascent of human beings in the evolutionary chain is furthermore at the cost of suffering to that wider kingdom. It gives evidence for the triumph of mind over matter referred to in Chapter 2. How, though, can the mind triumph ie make sense of the gravity of evil in humans, among animals and through natural disasters? Does suffering point us to heaven, where there is no suffering, only as reward or compensation? What sort of God in heaven could allow the suffering we see on earth?

Wrestling with such problems Timothy Keller points to an inconsistency among those who use suffering to shoot down belief in God and heaven. 'If you have a God great and transcendent enough to be mad at because he hasn't stopped evil and suffering in the world... you have... a God great and transcendent enough to have good reasons for allowing it to continue that you can't know... you can't have it both ways' (25). Suffering is beyond the human mind but once we accept the sovereignty of the mind of God we humble our questioning. This humbling is represented in scripture where we engage with the revelation of God in the face of suffering. The book of Job starts with a vivid picture of suffering that makes no sense until Job is granted a vision of God, in a glimmer half way through and in fullness at the end of the book where he actually repents of his questioning:

'I know that my Redeemer lives, and that at the last he will stand upon the earth; and after my skin has been thus destroyed, then in my flesh I shall see God... I know that you can do all things, and that no purpose of yours can be thwarted. "Who is this that hides counsel without knowledge?' Therefore I have uttered what I did not understand, things too wonderful for me, which I did not know. "Hear, and I will speak; I will question you, and you declare to me.' I had heard of you by the hearing of the ear, but now my eye sees you; therefore I despise myself, and repent in dust and ashes'. (Job 19:25-26, 42:2-6)

The suffering of Jesus

Job's vision of God reported in Chapter 42 is so awesome he drops the arguments of the previous 41 Chapters. In his Messiah the musician Handel built an inspiring solo from Job 19:25-26 as witness to Christ's resurrection. As we shall see in Chapter 9 this event is central to Christian belief in heaven. To say 'I know that my redeemer lives' is to affirm love's unconquerable might in the person of the risen Lord Jesus Christ. We see the Old Testament passage of Job 19 as fulfilled by the appearance of Christ after death which establishes the resurrection.

When Christ's disciples fled at his arrest and stood mainly at a distance for his crucifixion their disappointment in Christianity's Founder was evident. On the Emmaus road on Easter Day one spoke of 'Jesus of Nazareth, who was a prophet mighty in deed and word before God and all the people, and how our chief priests and leaders handed him over to be condemned to death and crucified him. But we had hoped that he was the one to redeem Israel' (Luke 24:19-21) The revelation to the disciples of the risen Jesus convinced them he was and is God's Son. His resurrection is so central to the emergence of Christianity that in Acts 17:18 Greek philosophers complain about Paul sharing 'about Jesus and the resurrection'. That disappointment in Christ's suffering was eclipsed by his resurrection is plain. Yet, Camus and others might ask, how can that resurrection provide a satisfactory ending to the human story given the enormity of suffering?

If at first the resurrection of Christ, and hope of the same for his followers, was centre stage for Christianity the New Testament contains highly significant interpretation of his death which shed light on suffering so as to challenge the pessimism about the meaning of life voiced by Camus and many through the ages.

'It is better to suffer for doing good, if suffering should be God's will, than to suffer for doing evil. For Christ also suffered for sins once for all, the righteous for the unrighteous, in order to bring you to God. He was put to death in the flesh, but made alive in the spirit.' (1 Peter 3:17-18) In those words scripture reveals how the capacity to suffer for others, here for God to bear the weight of our sins, makes of suffering a pointer to heaven. Christ's resurrection brings his accomplished work of love through suffering upon the Cross to all who will seize upon it in order to bring them to God over and above their unworthiness. Thomas was the first to literally seize hold of the risen Jesus crying 'my Lord and my God' after Christ showed him his wounded hands and side

(John 20:27-28). To this day Easter Candles lit in churches are imprinted with nails to represent Christ's wounds. An Advent hymn celebrates the same truth of the marks of Christ's suffering held in permanence:

> *Those dear tokens of his passion*
> *still his dazzling body bears,*
> *cause of endless exultation*
> *to his ransomed worshipers:*
> *with what rapture*
> *gaze we on those glorious scars!* (26)

If suffering is the greatest challenge to belief in God the revelation of God in Christ displays no aloofness, in contrast to other faiths, but God's coming down into it upon the Cross. In retaining his sacred wounds God in Christ brings us the assurance that there is nothing God expects of us that he has not been through before. A passage from Isaiah came to be seen in the light of the resurrection as a prophecy fulfilled in Christ's suffering on our behalf to carry our sins and alleviate our own suffering:

'He was despised and rejected by others; a man of suffering and acquainted with infirmity; and as one from whom others hide their faces he was despised, and we held him of no account. Surely he has borne our infirmities and carried our diseases; yet we accounted him stricken, struck down by God, and afflicted. But he was wounded for our transgressions and crushed for our iniquities; upon him was the punishment that made us whole, and by his bruises we are healed. All we like sheep have gone astray; we have all turned to our own way, and the Lord has laid on him the iniquity of us all.' (Isaiah 53:3-6)

In the light of this work of Christ CS Lewis writes not of suffering being a pointer to heaven as of heaven being a pointer back to illuminate earthly suffering: 'Heaven, once attained, will work backwards and turn...agony into a glory'. (27).

Seeking to bear suffering

The day my brother died in Brazil I was walking in a cemetery and something made me pause. A bright ray of sunshine struck a grave and in my mind's eye I imagined my brother and I beyond this world bathed in the glory of God. It was an extraordinary picture, in my mind, yes, but linked to something glorious outside of myself in that Belper cemetery. Tony was apparently on my heart and I had been thinking about him, in particular his reservations about my calling to full time Christian work about which I had a certain impatience. It was the following day that Tony's bank manger phoned me with the sad news of his death. This incident in the cemetery lay buried in my mind for a day or two with the tumult following that news, the sense of devastation shared by my mother and I and Tony's friends. To lose a loved one at their own hand brings uncomfortably close the traditional teaching that suicide cuts you off from God forever expressed in past exclusion of those who commit suicide from Christian funeral rites. When Christianity held total sway there was a policing of believers with punitive measures to deter wrong doing. The old practice linked to suicide saw the action of taking your life as so contemptuous of God as to be 'mortal sin', an action deadly to the soul, therefore needing the strongest deterrence. In the wake of Tony's death part my suffering was compounded by my Christian allegiance and the thought of Tony's sufferings being continued beyond death. When I eventually recalled that extraordinary picture of he and I one day in the glory of God I found enormous comfort in the pain of my bereavement.

I believe the experience of suffering and the supernatural are both pointers to heaven as surely as the pain of Tony's suicide and my hopeful vision of the two of us one day in heaven are woven into my life experience. Looking back I had impatience about our differences and within that there was always prayer to God for my brother to bring him fulfilment. Like many Tony had issues with the Church more than with God so my prayer for him was less for return to church membership than for an engagement with God who is living and true. If my prayer was impatient, in response to his impatience with my call to the priesthood, I dare to say it was a holy impatience in the sense of wanting the best for my brother. That God gave me a vision of the two of us in glorious fulfilment is an enormous consolation as for now I live life without Tony. 'The pains of life will be lost in the praise we sing' (28)

We all bear a degree of suffering in our dissatisfaction at the way the world is. This impatience relates to personal circumstances such as I have shared through to things that trouble our neighbourhood right across to the injustice in the world. No one seeks suffering directly but we can all seek to bear the sufferings that come to us personally and to those near and far on our hearts in the best way. Suffering breeds patience in those who accept it humbly as from the left hand of God. Some things we experience do not breed patience so much as godly impatience.

Why are people driven to take their lives? How can elderly people live for weeks without visitors? What in the world is driving so many to desperately leave their homelands as refugees? None of these questions have straightforward answers but asking them voices holy impatience at suffering in the world. Linked to asking is the questioner's readiness to invest in solutions like one-to-one conversations about mental health, befriending vulnerable neighbours and owning agencies devoted to building peace with justice in the world.

Sometimes our sufferings, or sympathy for others in theirs, breeds holy impatience that is transformative. As a priest I am made aware by many of their dissatisfaction at forms of worship both traditional and contemporary. I was recently involved in correspondence with an angry Latin-loving Catholic who felt marginalised in his parish where he found a lack of awe in worship and careless devotion with much talking before and during services. In our correspondence I found myself asking him to reflect on the importance of making the Eucharist accessible to irregular attenders and total outsiders given the decline of church attendance. How can your impatience at liturgical change be made more holy? Might the pain you feel be made part of the sacrificial offering we are called to make in union with Christ at the Eucharist especially for outsiders? As I wrote I felt for his priest who, as we shall consider in Chapter 10, has the awesome task of ensuring however accessible the service is people find in it a glimpse of heaven.

POINTERS TO HEAVEN - 7 VISIONS

Times when heaven breaks down upon earth

I have never seen God but there have been two occasions when I encountered him in a garden. The first came as I was reading the Sunday newspaper sitting in an Oxford garden after Church. I looked up at a tree and sensed these words addressed to me 'Go and see Ken Noakes'. I hardly knew Ken but he was a priest who lived across the road from me. At the time I was a Junior Fellow in Chemistry at St John's College and obeying the voice took me across the road to Pusey House. As a result of talking with Ken I crossed another road from Chemistry to Theology. Whether the voice was holy imagining or God speaking directly is second to the consequence. I packed my bags for my native Yorkshire to train as a priest.

Years later after ordination I was again halted whilst strolling in a Yorkshire garden. This time it was a leaf in a tree off the path which caught my attention. I stopped walking and waited on account of something extraordinary I sensed about the leaf. In due course I heard this from the leaf, outside or inside my mind, 'I made you. I love you. I want to fill you with my Spirit'. That became a word from God in answer to prayer in a faith crisis. Working as a priest had so drained me I felt God's absence to the extent I was close to quitting. I went back by instinct to the monastery at Mirfield where I had trained. Fr Daniel took me in hand. 'Maybe it's not God who's gone but your vision of God. Pray for a vision of God more to his dimensions and less to your own' was his advice.

The voice came in answer to a couple of days in prayer shaped by the monk's invitation. From that time, after receiving laying on of hands, I felt God not just around and above me but within me by his Spirit.

Through both of these experiences light shone down on me as if from above with great consequences. I felt heaven close to earth with my inner eyes opened to a reality beyond this world, to the living, loving God and his purpose for my life. Through an other-worldly vision I realised the hand of God upon my life and that life has this summary: we come from God, we belong to God and we go to God. Earth is in the midst of heaven, visible to the eye of faith, and God, in answer to prayer, chooses at times to reveal the full scene. Such visions are not guaranteed and, in my experience, have come at pivotal times to steer my life onto the right path for me or keep it where its meant to be when I get confused by doubt. Whereas those deceived by unbelief see faith as wishful thinking those possessing the sense of compulsion associated with faith press forward to nothing imagined but to what is promised and awaits all who so press on in hope, coming from, belonging to and going to God. As C.S.Lewis writes: 'A continual looking forward to the eternal world is not a form of escapism or wishful thinking, but one of the things a Christian is meant to do' (29)

I remember a stormy sea journey when at one point on our crossing of the Channel the sun broke through the storm clouds. Light streamed on the turbulent sea reflected forwards in a scene of extraordinary beauty. You could not look at the sun but you could feast on a remarkable display of light reflected from the moving waters. Their threatening look was changed into an inviting scene of immense beauty. So it is with the light of faith that invites us heavenwards through the storms of life awakening us to the vision of God as our final end.

Reason and revelation

As something God-given, faith is inevitably mysterious. Believers hold things together in their experience that live in tension from a rational perspective. Hence faith is seen as both a virtue and a gift, a human act yet one prompted by God, a personal act yet inseparable from the corporate faith of the church. The paradox of faith is captured in the famous definition of Thomas Aquinas: 'Believing is an act of the intellect assenting to the divine truth by command of the will moved by God through grace' (30). Though seen as a human virtue allied to determination, faith is also seen as something moved by God through grace. It marries reason and revelation, our seeking of heaven and heaven's seeking of us.

When I feel threatened by my circumstances I put faith in God. I ask for the light of faith in him to shine and change the look of things so I can persevere and do right. By that light I see beyond what's facing me outwardly to God's hand outstretched to me beyond those circumstances. In this way faith helps us see beyond our outward senses to the inward and heavenward movement. 'It is the God who said, "Let light shine out of darkness," who has shone in our hearts to give the light of the knowledge of the glory of God in the face of Jesus Christ' writes Paul in 2 Corinthians 4:6.

In the last chapter we reflected on how suffering and the supernatural are two poles of existence which are made pointers to heaven through Christ's suffering and resurrection. The heavenly appearances that most authenticate belief in heaven were provided by the risen Christ to around 500 people over a month or so after his crucifixion some time between 27-33 AD. As we shall consider in Chapter 9 the resurrection is central pointer to heaven on account of its public nature, objective albeit contested basis in world history which brought time to be measured from it. Through twenty centuries the risen Christ, his Mother Mary and other departed Christians have touched lives in a less publicly authenticated form. Some appearances like that of the Virgin Mary in Lourdes have received authentication from the Roman Catholic Church based on careful examination of the visionary Bernadette, many attested miracles and spiritual fruits of pilgrimage to Lourdes. The rigour of examination given at times to Christian visionaries is a reminder of how revelation and reason are interwoven. Without such examination visionaries claiming to relay messages from God or the saints could foster mindless credulity. On the other hand without openness to the supernatural Christianity would be untrue to its origins in the incarnation and resurrection of God in Christ and the supernatural gift of the Holy Spirit provided at Pentecost.

Belief in heaven is reasonable but it goes beyond reason. It is something revealed and to be further revealed by Jesus Christ. St John describes the ultimate purpose of our lives as purification so as to be capable of the vision of God for 'when he is revealed, we will be like him, for we will see him as he is'. (1 John 3:2b) At the hub of reality is God whose Son, as God and man, draws human beings into God's own self-contemplation, the Father of the Son in the Holy Spirit, catching us into God's own life so as to be energised. On earth vision of God is sporadic by people of faith in the midst of the uncoordinated chaos of life. In heaven saints purified from self-regard gaze in coordination upon the perfect goodness, truth and beauty of God. Through them, through the hub of their contemplation and intercession, God's power flows into the world. Contemplation in heaven and on earth leads to change, to transformation, from the image into the likeness of God as Paul makes clear in his second letter to Corinth: 'All of us, with unveiled faces, seeing the glory of the Lord as though reflected in a mirror, are being transformed into the same image from one degree of glory to another; for this comes from the Lord, the Spirit.' (2 Corinthians 3:18)

The vision of Jesus

In John's Gospel Jesus presents a vision of his destiny and the destiny of believers as a place: 'In my Father's house there are many mansions. If it were not so, would I have told you that I go to prepare a place for you? And if I go and prepare a place for you, I will come again and will take you to myself, so that where I am, there you may be also.' (John 14:2-3)

In these verses the Greek word *monai* translated as 'mansions' means literally resting-places or caravanserai. These were shelters at stages along the road where travellers might rest on their journey. Before the motor car it was customary in the Middle East for travellers to send a dragoman ahead to prepare the next resting-place for the caravan so that when the party arrived they might better comfort and shelter.

Here in this passage Jesus describes himself as a spiritual dragoman who treads the path before us, as what the letter to the Hebrews describes him: 'captain and perfecter of faith' (Hebrews 12:2).

Elsewhere in the Gospels Jesus speaks of heaven more as a relationship. He speaks of intimacy with God, of his and our Father in heaven, intimacy he invites his followers to share, one attained by his dying 'to gather into one the dispersed children of God' (John 11:52b). Jesus speaks more of eternal life than heaven and defines that life again as a personal relationship with God made possible by faith in him. 'This is eternal life, that they may know you, the only true God, and Jesus Christ whom you have sent' (John 17:3). In the letter of St John we read: 'God gave us eternal life, and this life is in his Son. Whoever has the Son has life; whoever does not have the Son of God does not have life.' (1 John 5:11-12) Accordingly the risen Christ makes this invitation in Revelation 3:20: 'Listen! I am standing at the door, knocking; if you hear my voice and open the door, I will come in to you and eat with you, and you with me'.

The artist Holman Hunt painted the last scene in his famous 'Light of the World' which now hangs in St Paul's Cathedral and Keble College, Oxford. In the painting Jesus stands holding a lamp before an ivy infested door in the act of knocking. The handle of what is presumed to represent the door of the human soul is on the inside presumed to be a dark house awaiting warmth and illumination. This painting captures the central invitation of Christianity to heavenly fellowship with God, something attained only as we open the door of our heart to the risen Lord Jesus. I was reminded of how real life this painting is when a fellow church member shared with me his testimony. Years back he attended Church but with no sense of God's love. One day he heard a sermon that encouraged the congregation to welcome Christ into their heart. After making such a prayer at his bedside he sensed the closeness of Jesus and this has never left him. My friend described the change in his life as if previously he had his back to the Lord. From the moment he welcomed Jesus he sensed the Lord no longer behind him but beside him leading him heavenwards.

In Matthew's Gospel Jesus presents heaven as a 'kingdom prepared for you from the foundation of the world'. In this passage he opens up a vision of heaven as once again about welcoming him but here in the person of needy people we recognise, welcome and serve. 'I was hungry and you gave me food, I was thirsty and you gave me something to drink, I was a stranger and you welcomed me, I was naked and you gave me clothing, I was sick and you took care of me, I was in prison and you visited me… Truly I tell you, just as you did it to one of the least of these who are members of my family, you did it to me. (Matthew 25:34-36, 40). In this passage Jesus confounds his listeners as he does so many times in his teaching in making plain the modest requirements needed to achieve greatness. Self-forgetful service is not forgotten by God in Christ to whom the first shall be last and the last first. His bias is towards the poor and needy and those with humility to come alongside them, qualities that equip us to be part of the communion of saints. 'A heaven of souls without Christ would not be heaven' Austin Farrer writes. 'Could we not say the same about a heaven of Christ without souls? Christ is not only God in man, he is God in mankind; God in one man isolated from all others would not even be God in man, for a man in isolation is not a human possibility' (31). The teaching of Jesus is about putting humanity into its right mind which challenges the individualism of our age: in the last resort there are two options, to have God in communion with others (heaven) or to have nothing but yourself.

Seeking a fuller vision of God

Although scripture observes that seeking signs from God can evidence weak faith it does nothing to discourage seeking an ever greater vision of God. In my faith crisis I was encouraged to do just that, to pray for a vision of God more to his dimensions and less to my own restricted vision. I prayed and God answered with an outpouring of his love. In consequence I have not hesitated to commend such a prayer to people who have approached me embarrassed by their own flagging faith. One day we will see God face to face. He has prepared us for this 'from the foundation of the world' (Matthew 25:34). Part of that preparation is expanding our vision as we gain insight from him through the fellowship of the church including the sort of spiritual direction I received in my faith crisis.

We grow our vision of God through worship, prayer, scripture, study of the saints and by turning to God in repentance. In these ways we also gain a fuller sense of who we are as his children, filled with his Spirit, promised his provision and destined for his glory. Seeing yourself more fully as God sees you is a real eye opener. It comes from a readiness to allow the opening up of those inner eyes that are the Spirit's gift to every human being, even if, mysteriously, so few seem graced to see them opened. Our aspiration for a fuller vision of God, like that of the saints in heaven, is never just our own. Paul asks in Ephesians that we may 'have power to comprehend, with all the saints, what is the breadth and length and height and depth... of ... the fullness of God' (Ephesians 3:18-19). In other words we only see God fully *together* with others. This has been my own experience in churches I have belonged to over the years which have usually had something intriguing about them. Sometimes it has been the rich variety of the membership ranging from shop workers to professors, home makers to colonels, Asian, African or Amerindian held together in worship.

What is it, this universal draw of the Christian church, what is its basis? Surely it is linked to a joy as out of this world as heaven! Children have this joy, Christ observed, as surely as they are humble, simple and trustful. What intrigues people about the church is when a local congregation is experienced as a joyous colony of heaven through an astonishing absence of pride. Alexander Schmemann, an Orthodox priest who lived and taught in New York in the late 20th century expands on this intriguing reality in a passage from his notebook about what he calls 'the 'I' passion of pride':

'Anything, one way or the other, even in microscopic dose, connected with pride, is connected with the devil and with the diabolical. Religion is a ready-made field of action for the devil's forces. Everything, absolutely everything in religion is ambiguous, and this ambiguity can be cleared only by humility, so that the whole spiritual life is or must be directed to seeking humility. The signs of humility: joy! Pride excludes joy. Then: simplicity, i.e., the absence of any turn into one's self. Finally, trust, as the main directive in life, applied to everything (purity of heart, when man can see God). The signs of pride are: the absence of joy; complexity and fear. All this can be verified every day, every hour, by watching one's self and contemplating life around.

'It is frightening to think that in some sense, the Church also lives with pride – 'the rights of the churches'…and a flood of joyless complicated and fearful spirituality. It is a continuous self-destruction. We try to protect the "Truth", we fight with something and for something without understanding that Truth appears and conquers only when it is alive: "humble yourself, be like a slave", and you will have a liberating joy and simplicity, where humility is radiant in its divine beauty; where God is revealed in creation and salvation. How can I live by this? How can I convince others?' (32)

'It is frightening to think that in some sense, the Church also lives with pride – 'the rights of the churches'...and a flood of joyless complicated and fearful spirituality. It is a continuous self-destruction. We try to protect the "Truth", we fight with something and for something without understanding that Truth appears and conquers only when it is alive: "humble yourself, be like a slave", and you will have a liberating joy and simplicity, where humility is radiant in its divine beauty; where God is revealed in creation and salvation. How can I live by this? How can I convince others?' (32)

POINTERS TO HEAVEN
- 8 PROMISES

Extrapolating God's faithful promises in scripture

I could never get into the Bible. Whenever I picked it up and started to read it my mind buzzed with critical analysis. This was a legacy of going to train for the ministry where emphasis in class was on putting the text of scripture in its historical context. I failed to pick up the devotional emphasis in Chapel where the Bible was honoured ceremonially and preaching unpacked from it a word of God for our contemporary situation. This changed after my experience of renewal in the Holy Spirit so that when I heard or read scripture there was a new expectancy upon God to speak personally through the words before me. Many a time when I read the Bible there's an invisible underlining of a phrase or verse almost the same as happens visibly when you highlight a text in word processing.

When I pick up Ephesians 1:3-6 for example it sometimes seems to read like this: 'Blessed be the God and Father of our Lord Jesus Christ, who has blessed *John* in Christ with every spiritual blessing in the heavenly places, just as he chose *John* in Christ before the foundation of the world to be holy and blameless before him in love. He destined *John* for adoption as his child through Jesus Christ, according to the good pleasure of his will, to the praise of his glorious grace that he freely bestowed on *John* in the Beloved'. I wonder if this makes sense to you as a reader, that scripture can read sometimes like a love letter from God with promises to you personally? It never read like that for me until I experienced the

Holy Spirit bringing the Bible alive to me. Another balancing act of God is guidance to pass over passages that bring me into useless mental gymnastics towards helpful words and phrases I see as written as if from God and as if for me personally or for those in my circle or situation.

I attend the eucharist most days where readings change day after day. Once I found the changes interesting at the level of the change of liturgical colour or saint of the day. Now I sit listening in apprehension knowing there is no word of God without power and that whatever is read can make a profound impact upon me. This is especially so when we read the Bible with other Christians, as Jesus made clear when he said 'where two or three are gathered in my name, I am there among them' (Matthew 18:20). I remember reading in Church once when my mother was staying with us the story of Jesus raising the widow of Naim's son which ends with the phrase 'he gave him to his mother' (Luke 7:15). It was as if I needed to go straightaway after service and sit down with my mother, which I did. I had to confess my inattention to her and be reconciled through sharing a leisurely conversation.

Scripture contains promises I have come to see as very relevant to my life, such as those concerning living in peace, guidance or answered prayer. All of these I am currently in a position to test and discover their truth. I am not yet in a position to test the promises about heaven but my experience so far of God's faithfulness to what he promises in scripture makes me utterly optimistic. With my scientific background I am familiar with testing theories by experiment eg plotting predicted graphs and seeing how close experimental data fit the curve. With the 'graph' of God's loving faithfulness I have experimental results as this book witnesses and they indeed fit close to the curve. Though I cannot yet test his promise of glory to come I am happy to extrapolate that curve in the spirit of the hymn writer John Newton:

> *Through many dangers, toils and snares, I have already come;*
> *'tis grace hath brought me safe thus far, and*

grace will lead me home. (33)

Revelation and reason

The Bible is a key pointer to heaven as record of God's dealings with his people. By reflecting back upon these we gain humility and confidence to cooperate with God into the future including a salvation beyond this world. The Old Testament is constructed around God's mighty act of deliverance of the Jews from captivity in Egypt, the Exodus. The New Testament addresses the universal captivity of sin and death through God's mighty saving act though the birth, death and resurrection of Jesus Christ. Unlike religious documents such as the Muslim Quran scripture is seen by mainstream Christianity as to be read contextually and interpreted consensually among believers through the ongoing authority of the Christian Church founded by Jesus Christ. This means Christian doctrine has seen development over the centuries, an unfolding of what is implied though not spelled out in scripture as in the doctrines of Christ's divinity, the Trinity, the atonement, eucharist, the last things etc.

Belief in life after death in Christianity links to belief in the resurrection of its Founder which we will consider in the next Chapter. It also links to the promise of salvation beyond this world that thrills through the New Testament. Salvation - attaining heaven - is promised as a gift and a task.

If we saw the dawn more often we might be better at seeing life as the gift it is. Sunrise each day is the grand reminder of the gift of life. All that we are is given from beyond this world. Life is both a gift and a task. It's no good taking the gift and doing nothing with it. Today is given so we can make a difference to the world, and build God's kingdom of truth and holiness, justice, love and peace. Pity those, however, for whom life is just a task, who live in drudgery for whom today is just another lifeless routine. Evangelisation is about opening such folk up to the wonder of God's overall gift as we come from him, belong to him and go to him.

Life is both a gift and a task. 'Work out your own salvation with fear and trembling' writes Paul 'for it is God who is at work in you, enabling you both to will and to work for his good pleasure' (Philippians 2:12b-13).

We live our lives as believers like workmen building a concrete path. They construct a wooden frame by their own efforts and then they pour in concrete. So it is with Christian life. We accept it as a task and we also accept it as a gift, so that very often we see God completing our task to make it solid, like concrete poured into a wooden frame. So it is with the gift of eternal life which is heaven, something mortal beings cannot possess without a gift from the immortal giver of life and salvation.

Though we cannot say precisely *what* happens after death the promises of scripture affirm *who* is there in the person of God and the saints he holds in immortal life 'for God so loved the world that he gave his only Son, so that everyone who believes in him may not perish but may have eternal life' (John 3:16). Christian tradition distinguishes an individual judgement at the moment of death and a general judgement which completes God's righteous task at the Lord's return when the dead are raised in body as well as soul. After death scripture speaks of two ultimate destinies, heaven and hell, although there is a qualification that no one dying with unrepented sin can face the Lord without cleansing, since 'nothing unclean' shall enter his presence (Revelation 21:27). This is the origin of the doctrine of purgatory which speaks of the need for the faithful departed to be purged or cleansed of residual sin to come close to God.

The promises of Jesus

The promises of Jesus are balanced by his challenges. When we first read Christ's sermon on the mount heaven begins to look far off though his wake up call to perfection. 'I tell you, unless your righteousness exceeds that of the scribes and Pharisees, you will never enter the kingdom of heaven'. No wonder at one point, faced with people turning away from their Lord, the disciples protested 'who can be saved?' to which he responded in typically enigmatic fashion 'for mortals it is impossible, but for God all things are possible'. Being saved so we can go to heaven is not something we can accomplish ourselves, Jesus implies. It is something God must do for us. (Matthew 5:20, 19:25-26)

Salvation, Jesus promises, is both a gift and a struggle. Faced with the spiritual complacency of the religious leaders of his day he issues shocking indictments of hypocrisy. At the same time he makes gracious promises like these: 'Come to me, all you that are weary and are carrying heavy burdens, and I will give you rest. Take my yoke upon you, and learn from me; for I am gentle and humble in heart, and you will find rest for your souls. For my yoke is easy, and my burden is light." (Matthew 11:28-30) Again in John 6:37b and Revelation 22:17b: 'anyone who comes to me I will never drive away... let everyone who is thirsty come. Let anyone who wishes take the water of life as a gift.' 'This is eternal life' we read in John 17:3 'to know God and Jesus Christ whom he has sent'. To be saved is to welcome intimacy with the Creator who's shown himself in Jesus Christ, a never ending and ever deepening relationship with all the saints.

What does it mean to be saved? The promises of God in scripture imply it is to have assurance about God's love for you and for all shown in the death and resurrection of Jesus. 'Believe on the Lord Jesus and you will be saved' (Acts 16:31) is the invitation of the Christian faith leading into an adventure that is personal, practical, purposeful and out of this world. To be saved is to know God personally and experience his practical provision to put you more on your feet - and for a purpose. That purpose is the transformation of the universe as it is gathered under the reign of Christ including the populating of heaven.

To be saved heading for heaven is to have made your life purpose one with the saving work of God announced by his Son Jesus Christ establishing his kingdom of justice, mercy, peace for which the creation itself yearns. We are saved to serve and be part of this aspiration in our deeds and also in our words of witness. Salvation places us under the authority of Jesus who gave us this great commission: 'Go and make disciples of all nations, baptizing them in the name of the Father and of the Son and of the Holy Spirit, and teaching them to obey everything that I have commanded you'. (Matthew 28:19-20)

Seeking what God promises

In promising heaven scripture promises judgement as its gateway. Our minds argue against judgement because they think they know best even if the instinct of faith within us recognises God knows best in the end. When we look into the eyes of Christ at his return there will be pain, but an 'if the cap fits wear it' sort of pain. Purgatorial pain may be as short as that. Our wrong actions affront God in his holiness but he has given us a remedy in repentance. Hell, refusal to face God, will be our choice. As the video of my life is prepared for showing on judgement day Christ has power to edit out the unacceptable points if I give them to him. Mercy triumphs over judgement when we allow Christ a place in our hearts!

'There is no condemnation for those who are in Christ Jesus' we read in Romans 8:1. God looks on those who are in Christ with the same love with which he looks upon his Son. Judgement has in a profound sense been passed already for those who have accepted God's judgement on their lives. To accept one's sinfulness and inadequacy is in the Christian tradition the pathway to joyful freedom. Such acceptance springs from the vision of God given in Jesus Christ we celebrate at every eucharist, vision of a God of majesty, yes, but also a God more concerned to give us what we need than to give us what we deserve. To believe in Jesus Christ who 'will come to judge the living and the dead' is therefore to face the future with an infectious hope. If faith shows you that the whole world is in God's hands *so is its future.* (34)

How then do we best follow the pointers to heaven? Keep 'in Christ Jesus' away from condemnation? What strategies do we need to realise the fulfilment of God's promises in our lives? Jesus promises an easy yoke and rest to all who come to him 'weary and carrying heavy burdens' but what exactly is that yoke?

Just as reading the Bible became easier for me after opening my life more to God's Spirit so we can refashion a rule of life in the power of the Holy Spirit that is our servant not our tyrant. In my book 'Experiencing Christ's Love' I present such a rule of Christian discipleship.

'As I prayed for God-given competence to write this book the Lord drew me to an image of his hand reaching down to me and my own hand grasping his with its five digits expressing *five loves* commended in Christ's summary of the Old Testament Law in Matthew 22:37-39: 'You shall love the Lord your God with all your heart, and with all your soul, and with all your mind.' This is the greatest and first commandment. And a second is like it: 'You shall love your neighbour as yourself'. In this teaching, his so-called Summary of the Law, Jesus implies that *worship* and *prayer* are to be seen as heart and soul of our love for God. He implies, though, that without *study* engaging the mind with divine teaching that love will be ill formed, and without *service*, love of neighbour, and *reflection*, loving care of self, our loving God is a delusion. Those five commitments - worship, prayer, study, service, reflection - make for me a hand that can grasp the hand of God reaching down to us in Jesus Christ to raise us into his praise and service with all the saints, an image of the grace (or favour) of God towards us.' (35)

The five loves invited by Jesus in Matthew 22:37-39 are a call to and a reminder of balanced and effective discipleship. What's distinctive about Christian as opposed to other spiritual disciplines is the 'hand up' of grace they engage with. If Christian disciplines attain salvation they do so by grasping the hand of the

Saviour. Experiencing Christ's love in the five disciplines of worship, prayer, study, service and reflection is a taking of God's hand in ours, the welcoming of his loving provision of forgiveness and healing that's a hand up into his possibilities. Worship, prayer, study, service and reflection are balanced disciplines. When two or three fail we keep grasp, or rather the Lord retains grasp of us, through what's still directed to him in the conduct of our lives. Study and reflection are particularly vital aids in challenging very many deceptions around us and within us. Through them our worship gains heart through understanding, our prayer gets kindled as God's word comes alive to us and our service is made more effective by our better discerning what God requires of us. In this way in all our frailty we are brought to know the love of Christ passing knowledge with its downward (God to us), upward (us to God) and outward (God and us to the world) aspects.

Christians live under grace with a big aim – God's glory and the world's salvation – and a tight focus expressed as they worship on Sunday, pray every day, study the Bible, serve their neighbour and reflect upon their lives confessing their sins. The ultimate experience of Christ's love will be in heaven and as we recognise that and seek the fulfilment it will bring we have hour by hour motivation to hold ourselves close to the Lord. This means checking self-will so that our time is consecrated through these basic and balanced spiritual disciplines. Seeking what God promises is a task, yes, but it is also a grace from above since we come from God, we belong to God and we go to God. More profoundly it is a taking of God at his word in his scripture promises, an act of confidence that he will complete his work within us, within the church and within creation to bring everything together in Christ.

'May you know the love of Christ that surpasses knowledge, so that you may be filled with all the fullness of God' (Ephesians 3:19).

POINTERS TO HEAVEN
- 9 RESURRECTION

Jesus Christ the same yesterday, today and always

A highlight in my life was getting my atheist friend Clive in on the launch of the Premier Christian Radio 'Unbelievable?' programme which was great fun with the predominantly Christian audience quizzing and challenging my friend. Usually the experience is more in reverse with Christians in the UK at the sharp end on account of their faith. It is good that Justin Brierley presents a level platform one afternoon a week on Premier Radio when atheists and believers can clarify their thinking and lose their prejudices (36). I regularly present and debate Christianity on radio and social media and at the centre of that engagement is engaging with folk about the resurrection of Jesus.

'No thoughtful Christian can allow the Resurrection to be placed in one category with any other class of event' Austin Farrer wrote, 'any more than he can allow God to be placed in one category with any other class of being' (37). God as God who raises the dead is pivotal to thinking about God in Christ and the supreme Christian pointer to heaven. In my conversations with atheists one issue has been clarifying the God we believe or disbelieve in. On occasion I have agreed with my atheist friend's disbelief because the God they rejected was implausible and unscriptural! If God exists, as Farrer says, he is not just another being but someone in whom all creatures 'live and move and have their being' (Acts 17:28). The God and Father of Jesus furthermore puts himself into history by revealing the realm beyond death through Christ's resurrection and humanity is left to weigh the evidence. I find it helpful to look at the case for the resurrection on a par with the case for the Big Bang. There's no hard proof just enough circumstantial findings to make belief reasonable to an averagely intelligent human being. Richard Dawkins makes robust defence of atheism in 'The God Delusion' but his persistent refusal to debate the resurrection is telling (38). As a naturalist he is less equipped than a historian and few historians altogether dismiss the resurrection. Indeed many would say belief in the historical basis of the New Testament has been strengthened rather than weakened by academic scrutiny over 200 years.

The 40 days preparing for Easter we call Lent are balanced by a festive season of 40 days afterwards based on Acts 1:3 where we read 'after Christ's suffering he presented himself alive to his disciples by many convincing proofs, appearing to them during forty days'. I made it my challenge in Lent 2018 to prepare 40 pointers to Christ's resurrection to release daily in Easter Season via a blog on Instagram, Twitter and Facebook using 40 classic paintings of the risen Lord with 100 word captions setting forth evidence for the truth of Easter. This blog can be accessed on the internet. It summarises to an extent a month long debate I had some years back with an atheist prominent on social media who wanted someone to take on about the truth of the resurrection (39).

Though Christ proved his resurrection to the first disciples over 40 days we must rest with pointers to its truth. There's no knock down proof of any event alleged to have happened in the past. You have just got to weigh the evidence. Hard evidence for an event that happened in a relatively primitive society 2000 years is not likely. Even if we had written testimony - and we have close to that - it would be disputed as imaginary, just as events videoed and photographed today are regularly disputed as forgeries. When you look at the resurrection of Jesus on Wikipedia most of the text relays it as an attested event but there is this qualifying section: 'The historicity and origin of the resurrection of Jesus has been the subject of historical research and debate, as well as a topic of discussion among theologians. The accounts of the Gospels, including the empty tomb and the appearances of the risen Jesus to his followers, have been interpreted and analyzed in diverse ways, and have been seen variously as historical accounts of a literal event, as accurate accounts of visionary experiences, as non-literal eschatological parables, and as fabrications of early Christian writers, among various other interpretations' (40).

Revelation and reason

We have seven great pointers to heaven - accounts of Christ's Resurrection - in the New Testament. These accounts are at the heart of the Christian revelation of God in Christ but they have a rational rather than a fanciful basis. Textual critics have yet to undermine the complementary witness of Mark 16:1-8, Matthew 28, Luke 24, John 20 and Mark 16:9-13, Acts 1:1-11 and 1 Corinthians 15:3-8. There are inconsistencies in geography and timing but in recording an event stretching the boundaries of space and time that is unsurprising. It has not deterred the ongoing digestion of these passages over centuries and their acceptance by eminent historians. The discrepancies in the passages point to there having been little management in recording what happened. A made-up story would be neater. The basic agreement between accounts evidences their recording from different angles the same mind-blowing event.

The whole thrust of St. Paul's writings, the earliest Christian documentation, is that Jesus Christ was and is raised as first born of the dead (Romans 4:24f, 6:4, 6:9, 7:4, 8:11, 29, 34, 10:9; 1 Corinthians 6:14, 15:4, 12-17, 20, 29, 32, 35, 42-44, 52; 2 Corinthians 1:9, 4:14, 5:15; Galatians 1:1; Ephesians 1:20; Colossians 2:12; 1 Thessalonians 1:10). Critical biblical scholarship has established these Pauline texts as earliest evidence of the resurrection followed by the later gospel narratives. At the heart of Paul's gospel is the desire to safeguard the historical facts central to Christianity: 'I hand it on to you as of first importance what I in turn have received: that Christ died for our sins in accordance with the Scriptures, and that he was buried, and that he was raised on the third day in accordance with the scriptures' (1 Corinthians 15:3-4). This core gospel statement has four parts stressing Christ's burial. Paul professes here the resuscitation of Christ's buried corpse and the emptying of his tomb. In my online debate with my atheist friend his prime difficulty was in accepting Paul's witness to the resurrection as being more than subjective i.e. unrelated to the accounts of the empty tomb found in the slightly later Gospel narratives. Tom Wright addresses this suggesting multiple lines of evidence from the New Testament and the early Christian beliefs it reflects show it would be highly unlikely that belief in the empty tomb would simply appear without a clear basis in the memory of the early Christians (41).

As previously noted a concerted plot to foster belief in the resurrection of Jesus would probably have resulted in a more consistent story. It is not in question among scholars that the followers of Jesus with Paul had experience of what became known as the resurrection. What is at issue to this day is whether those resurrection experiences were non-material visions i.e. subjective in their minds or based on objective appearances of Jesus Christ risen from the dead and discovery of his tomb being empty. With the repeated witness of the Gospel accounts to the latter it seems difficult to deny that the earliest conception of resurrection in the first Christian community was objective i.e. physical.

In first-century Israel, women were not allowed to testify in a court of law as they were considered unreliable witnesses. Yet the New Testament accounts of Christ's Resurrection indicate how in seeking to get news of this out to the world he commissioned women followers, chiefly Mary Magdalene, to do it. This choice is in harmony with the esteem Jesus had for women. The role of women as witnesses is remarkable and controversial for those days and would not have been included in any fabricated story.

Study of the Gospels and the Acts of the Apostles shows how Christ's disciples changed from a sad defeated group into fearless missionaries. Peter in particular evidently denied he knew Christ before a servant girl who challenged him after the arrest of Jesus. Weeks later the same man could not be silenced by the whole Jewish Sanhedrin where he gave a fearless witness to the resurrection. There's a strong tradition Peter was martyred for his faith in Christ as unique Saviour, crucified yet risen from the dead.

The Jewish Sabbath from Friday night gave way for Christians to Sunday as the Lord's Day. Not only were the first disciples changed by encounter with the risen Lord Jesus, the very day of weekly worship got changed. This is a fact of history which needs accounting for given the conservatism of religious traditions, especially Judaism which keeps the same regulations today as in Jesus' day for the commencement of Sabbath on Friday evening. Christ's Resurrection 'on the third day' is allegedly behind this change.

The resurrection of Jesus

The earliest Gospel, that of Saint Mark, ends with this succinct account of the resurrection of Jesus:

'When the sabbath was over, Mary Magdalene, and Mary the mother of James, and Salome bought spices, so that they might go and anoint [the body of Jesus]. And very early on the first day of the week, when the sun had risen, they went to the tomb. They had been saying to one another, "Who will roll away the stone for us from the entrance to the tomb?" When they looked up, they saw that the stone, which was very large, had already been rolled back. As they entered the tomb, they saw a young man, dressed in a white robe, sitting on the right side; and they were alarmed. But he said to them, "Do not be alarmed; you are looking for Jesus of Nazareth, who was crucified. He has been raised; he is not here. Look, there is the place they laid him. But go, tell his disciples and Peter that he is going ahead of you to Galilee; there you will see him, just as he told you." So they went out and fled from the tomb, for terror and amazement had seized them; and they said nothing to anyone, for they were afraid.' (Mark 16:1-8)

Scholars separate this bald account from the remaining eleven verses of Mark's Gospel seen as additions from other sources than Mark himself. The passage captures the wonder and initial terror of Easter Sunday with its uncomfortable last words 'they were afraid' which might have been caused by loss of the end of Mark's parchment. New Testament editors add reassuring accounts of the risen Christ's encounters with Mary Magdalene and others. This is like the editors' work around the Lord's Prayer. In earliest accounts this ends with 'deliver us from the evil one' but in the footnote to Matthew 6:13 we read 'Other ancient authorities add, in some form, 'For the kingdom and the power and the glory are yours for ever. Amen'.

That the ending of a Gospel - book of good news - like that of a prayer to God should be upbeat is instinctive. That death and the devil need countering in text as well as reality is the logic here and that is quite intelligible. The resurrection of Jesus turns both death and the devil on their heads! Peter Kreeft's book Love is Stronger than Death explores five faces of death. Death, he says, is seen firstly by instinct as an enemy. As life and faith deepen, it turns from enemy into the more neutral face of a stranger. By the gift of faith death becomes friend, mother and, finally, lover. In what Kreeft calls this incredible divine judo God in Jesus has turned his opponent's own strongest force and momentum against him. Death as enemy and Satan's instrument of destruction is on Easter Sunday turned head over heels by divine judo into a friend! (42)

Each one of us has a terminal illness and life is either totally meaningless or totally meaningful, depending on the vantage point we have on that fact. Thornton Wilder paints the dilemma of two vantage points, one without and one with the perspective of the resurrection of Jesus: 'Some say that...to the gods we are like the flies that boys kill on a summer day. And some say, on the contrary, that the very sparrows do not lose a feather that has not been brushed away by the finger of God' (43). What we see about death depends upon our vantage point. The atheist Bertrand Russell had this to say about life and death: 'There is darkness without, and when I die there will be darkness within. There is no splendour, no vastness anywhere, only triviality for a moment and then nothing' (44). Contrast this sad vision of death with a statement of resurrection faith from the writings of the nineteenth century theologian Kohlbrugge who once imagined someone finding his skull a century later: 'When I die - I do not die anymore, he wrote. If someone finds my skull, let this skull still preach to him and say: I have no eyes, nevertheless I see Him; though I have no lips, I kiss him; I have no tongue, yet I sing praise to Him with all who call upon His name. I am a hard skull, yet I am wholly softened and melted in His love…All suffering is forgotten' (45). In that wonderful statement of resurrection faith the 'enemy' is made a friend. His power is turned to our good, so that St. Francis could give death an honoured place in his great hymn of creation: 'And thou, most kind and gentle death/waiting to hush our latest breath./Thou leadest home the child of God,/ and Christ our Lord the way hath trod/alleluia' (46)

Seeking resurrection

If I accept the pointers to heaven, supremely the resurrection of Jesus, how can I seek and reach that destination?

The resurrection of Jesus opens up a country beyond this world hidden until his coming which seeks a population of people beyond this world i.e. holy people fit for fellowship with God, Father, Son and Holy Spirit. Jesus made clear his resurrection is the first fruits of that greater harvest. To seek and find heaven is inseparable from seeking and finding holiness for without that no one is fit to see God. It is linked to seeking and finding what scripture calls 'salvation'. A practical guide is given in questions put to and answered by Christ's apostles:

'Brothers what should we do? Peter said to them, "Repent, and be baptized every one of you in the name of Jesus Christ so that your sins may be forgiven; and you will receive the gift of the Holy Spirit. For the promise is for you, for your children, and for all who are far away, everyone whom the Lord our God calls to him."(Acts 2:37b-39)

'"Sirs, what must I do to be saved?" [Paul and Silas] answered, "Believe on the Lord Jesus, and you will be saved, you and your household."(Acts 16:30b-31)

Christianity - resurrection - salvation - starts in someone when they repent of their sins, put faith in Jesus as Lord and Saviour and ask for and receive the Holy Spirit through baptism into the Church.

'So if you have been raised with Christ, seek the things that are above, where Christ is, seated at the right hand of God. Set your minds on things that are above, not on things that are on earth, for you have died, and your life is hidden with Christ in God. When Christ who is your life is revealed, then you also will be revealed with him in glory. Put to death, therefore, whatever in you is earthly: fornication, impurity, passion, evil desire, and greed... As God's chosen ones, holy and beloved, clothe yourselves with compassion, kindness, humility, meekness, and patience... Above all, clothe yourselves with love, which binds everything together in perfect harmony. And let the peace of Christ rule in your hearts, to which indeed you were called in the one body. And be thankful. Let the word of Christ dwell in you richly; teach and admonish one another in all wisdom; and with gratitude in your hearts sing psalms, hymns, and spiritual songs to God' (Colossians 3:1-5, 12, 14-16).

POINTERS TO HEAVEN
- 10 WORSHIP

With angels and archangels and all the company of heaven

It was a memorable eucharist in Westminster Abbey with young and old, bishops, priests among a thousand worshippers at a celebration of the Blessed Virgin Mary. As the clergy procession entered trumpets sounded, the choir started the entrance anthem after which the congregation burst into a hymn of praise. The Bishop ascended the coronation altar in front of St Edward the Confessor's shrine amidst clouds of incense.

As this awesome service proceeded I imagined the departed whose shrines adorn the Abbey looking over our shoulders as the Bishop intoned the consecration prayer of the eucharist joined by the choir, 'therefore with angels and archangels and with , we proclaim your great and glorious name, for ever praising you and singing 'Holy, holy, holy Lord, God of power and might, heaven and earth are full of your glory. Hosanna in the highest. Blessed is he who comes in the name of the Lord. Hosanna in the highest... this is my body, which is given for you... my blood... shed for you... we offer you... our sacrifice of praise and thanksgiving' (47)

Westminster Abbey can feel a shrine of self-importance with many epitaphs of that sort. The Abbey's inclusive yet distinctive Christian worship runs counter in affirming God as the one in whom we find significance. With its regal grandeur the building points beyond and above itself. The words inscribed over the high altar jumped out at me that morning: 'the kingdoms of this world are become the kingdom of our Lord and of his Christ' (Revelation 11:15b) That day they were not just aspiration but touched on reality there and then as hundreds did business with God with the nation on our hearts.

Every eucharist is a pointer from earth to heaven, an earthly meal anticipating the heavenly banquet. On that day I felt part of a vast communion of worship overlooked and supported by 'angels and archangels and all the company of heaven' in acknowledging the wonder and splendour of God. It was a loss of myself to become part of the grand unity of the church, the community of the risen Lord Jesus stretching beyond church walls into eternity, living with lives gained meaning by the conquest of death. At the heart of my worship that day was a sense of uplift linked to the lifting up of Christ on the Cross to draw others upwards and onwards to extend the reign of God on earth as it is in heaven. The lifting up of the Gospel book by the deacon and the consecrated Bread and Wine by the bishop linked to the congregation's act of self-offering for the praise and service of God.

Christian worship is the supreme pointer to heaven though often dull and dry in earthly terms. That morning in Westminster Abbey what we were about was exceptional in my experience helping feed my faith through imagination to see the fuller reality of what happens in worship. There was a sense of the angels making space in their choirs for our worship, grand in earthly measure yet feeble in heavenly terms. Our common ground, in earthly terms, was the foot of Christ's Cross. In heavenly terms that base was Christ the 'Lamb slain from the foundation of the world' whose worship is vividly described in the last book of the Bible:

'Then I looked, and I heard the voice of many angels surrounding the throne and the living creatures and the elders; they numbered myriads of myriads and thousands of thousands, singing with full voice, "Worthy is the Lamb that was slaughtered to receive power and wealth and wisdom and might and honor and glory and blessing!" Then I heard every creature in heaven and on earth and under the earth and in the sea, and all that is in them, singing, "To the one seated on the throne and to the Lamb be blessing and honor and glory and might forever and ever!'" (Revelation 5:11-13, 13:8)

Revelation and reason

Our reasoning powers trace experiences of goodness, truth, beauty, holiness and love to find in them pointers to heaven. Suffering and visions point us beyond reason to otherworldly fulfilment. The promises of scripture, the resurrection of Jesus and worship contain what is revealed by God in Jesus Christ which we could never reason out for ourselves. Many a time worship in my experience becomes the place for ceasing argument with God and *letting God be God!* There are many things in life like the Coronavirus pandemic which unsettle our reason in the face of belief in the goodness of God. In worship, on earth as in heaven, we *let God be God* accepting what is revealed of him in the face of Jesus crucified and confess how partial our perception of things is unaided by divine revelation. Offering the eucharist during the pandemic brought home to me how the anguish of the world was and is and always will be enfolded in the joyous love of God shown upon the Cross, a love expecting nothing of us that it would shrink back from itself.

In his book 'Spirit and Sacrament' Andrew Wilson quotes G.K.Chesterton: 'Man is more himself when joy is the fundamental thing in him, and grief the superficial. Melancholy should be an innocent interlude, a tender and fugitive frame of mind; praise should be the permanent pulsation of the soul... the tremendous figure which fills the Gospels towers in that respect'. Wilson affirms how divine joy and intimacy with Christ in hardship are inseparable from participation in the Eucharist. He reasons towards a church capturing the best of both worlds, charismatic and sacramental through recapturing the centrality of God's grace in worship and discipleship. Wilson coins the amalgam 'eucharismatic', playing on the Greek 'gracious' origin of both 'eucharist' and 'charism', to counter and bid expansion of narrowness in both worship traditions. The more liturgical churches resonate with the worship of the church through the ages but can lack exuberant praise just as Pentecostalism with all its exuberance can shrink away from sacraments through unease with their age-old formality. Andrew Wilson looks to the 'eucharismatic' church of the future in which 'the triune God is experienced... through the physical symbols of bread, wine and water, through the Word read and proclaimed, and the presence of the Holy Spirit among us' (48)

Reflecting in response to Wilson on how worship other than eucharistic has revealed something of heaven to me I recall in my book 'Meet Jesus' an encounter with singing in tongues:

'I well remember visiting out of interest a charismatic service in St Matthias Church in Leeds in the 1970s, the early days of the [charismatic] movement in the UK. As I came through the door, a late arrival, I heard a loud harmonious singing without intelligible words. My instinct was to fall to my knees, because I was hearing something awesome, quite out of this world. Such was my first experience of singing in tongues. What impressed me was that unlike liturgical prayer this worship had no evident human organisation but rose to a crescendo, flowed on for several minutes and then ceased reverently, producing a deep silence. Speaking in tongues is one of a number of supernatural gifts or charisms (hence 'charismatic') like healing, miracles, prophecy and so on, listed in 1 Corinthians 12 and elsewhere which can be exercised in worship. In charismatic worship people receive words of guidance, healings and reminders of God's love for them from the Holy Spirit, which can bear fruit in a closer relationship with Jesus. By reputation, charismatic worship is noisy but the essence of it is about receiving an encouraging touch or word or vision from the Holy Spirit, which very often takes place in silences that punctuate free worship' (49).

Christian worship in all its variety and inadequacy engages with a fullness more enduring than hymns, texts, sacraments or tongues which permeates those words and actions. Divine love took flesh to point us to and draw us into the worship which existed before the world was made and will continue when the world has crumbled to dust.

The worship of Jesus

During the coronavirus pandemic my church prayed morning and evening prayer by audio conference. This meant voices on the phone in locations across Mid Sussex were employed in sequence to read the psalms, canticles, scripture readings and prayers as we all followed the text on the internet. It reminded me how in taking flesh God the Son has brought voices even beyond this world to join with us in worship. 'Christ Jesus, high priest of the new and eternal covenant, taking human nature, introduced into this earthly exile that hymn which is sung throughout all ages in the halls of heaven' (50). The solidarity of Christian worship with worship beyond this world is a most powerful pointer to that world opened up to believers in the person of Jesus Christ, truly God and truly human.

When we read the Gospels we are struck by the teaching and practice of Jesus on worship. It was 'his custom' (Luke 4:16) to attend synagogue worship and the temple in Jerusalem was his 'house of prayer' (Matthew 21:13). His repeated call for the purification of worship reflects his origin in 'the halls of heaven' where the sight of God unveiled is the privilege of saints and angels. 'Blessed are the pure in heart' he said 'for they shall see God' (Matthew 5:8). The anger of Jesus against hypocrisy is rooted in such purity. Worship to Jesus is about both ritual and life so that he once advised: 'When you are offering your gift at the altar, if you remember that your brother or sister has something against you, leave your gift there before the altar and go; first be reconciled to your brother or sister, and then come and offer your gift' (Matthew 5:23-24)

The coronavirus pandemic revealed the solidarity of humankind for better and for worse. The flow of altruism linked to a profound sense of solidarity in need. The flow of self-interest and of the virus itself reminded us how earth falls short of heaven through sin and sickness. In the days of his flesh Jesus applauded human solidarity whilst calling it into the worship of God through countering sin, sickness, death and the devil at supreme cost to himself. He died 'to gather into one the dispersed children of God' (John 11:52b). Such unity, foretaste of heaven on earth, was established by his bringing the prayer of heaven to earth. 'In the days of his flesh, Jesus offered up prayers and supplications, with loud cries and tears, to the one who was able to save him from death, and he was heard because of his reverent submission' (Hebrews 5:7). At his death 'the curtain of the temple was torn in two' (Mark 15:38) sign of Jesus opening heaven's worship to all and not just an élite. Risen from the dead 'he is able for all time to save those who approach God through him, since he always lives to make intercession for them... for by a single offering he has perfected for all time those who are sanctified' (Hebrews 7:25, 10:14)

Jesus Christ's institution of the worship of the eucharist contains these sacrificial words: 'This is my body that is for you... this cup is the new covenant in my blood. Do this, as often as you drink it, in remembrance of me'. Paul adds an interpretation of this worship: 'For as often as you eat this bread and drink the cup, you proclaim the Lord's death until he comes' (1 Corinthians 11:24-26). In the previous chapter the Apostle has challenged idolatry among the Corinthians and in so doing spoken by way of contrast of the godly eucharistic sacrifice. 'Pagans sacrifice to demons and not to God... you cannot drink the cup of the Lord and the cup of demons' (1 Corinthians 10:20-21). Paul's phrase quoted earlier 'proclaiming [or showing] the Lord's death' is a powerful summary of the implication of the separate consecration and receiving of bread and wine which John Wesley saw as 'a converting ordinance'. (51). Showing the Lord's death to God on behalf of the cosmos has been understood not only as anticipating but as expediting Christ's return. To Paul we also owe the understanding of Christians being Christ's Body of which Christ is the head and God's call to believers 'to present your bodies as a living sacrifice, holy and acceptable to God, which is your spiritual worship' (Romans 12:1b). This last call is taken up in Christian devotion where the eucharistic sacrifice is seen as both Christ's and ours.

Seeking worship

You don't need to go to Westminster Abbey as I did to get pointed to heaven. Worship links to places but it's primarily about people. Heaven is less a place than a gathering of the pure in heart.

Seeking worship is more about renewing hearts than finding outward forms or places. Impatience with forms of worship can be godly, but it can also be ungodly. It's a godly motive to make worship accessible to outsiders. It's ungodly to make worship bespoke. Bespoke is all the rage, such as bespoke clothing custom made to your own specification, as opposed to a ready to wear item. Bespoke is now no longer just about tailored clothing. It's about all sorts of things. Worship though cannot be bespoke. It's the very opposite. The Anglo Saxon means to give worth to something beyond you. Worship is the adoring acknowledgment of One beyond sight whose glory fills heaven and earth - very 'unbespoke'!

Heaven breaks into earthly worship when participants centre on God rather than self. The word adoration means from the Greek 'submission' and from the Latin 'ad-oratio', literally, mouth to mouth, the kiss of love. Seeking true worship is about building our individual submission and loving devotion to God through prayer, bible study, service and reflection. These aspects of devotion as orient to God, neighbour and self so we approach worship in love for God, knowing our need of him and with the needy in our acquaintance upon our hearts before God.

Seeing such profundity - a pointer to heaven - beyond brief action with scripture, bread and wine is the gift of catechesis and engagement with holy people who over the course of my life have for me lifted the veil covering the sacred mysteries of the eucharist. In recognising the power of Christ's sacrificial prayer to which my intentions are joined day by day I have gained confidence in a transformative dynamic summarised in Our Lord's promise that 'I, when I am lifted up from the earth, will draw all people to myself' (John 12:32). All people, but also *all things* as St Paul writes of all things being ultimately put 'in subjection under Christ, so that God may be all in all' (1 Corinthians 15:28). Such ultimately is the power of the eucharist which is Christ's means of bringing the world into what he wants it to be. So many times I have been able to look back days or weeks later at the fulfilment of intentions I have taken to the eucharist even concerning world crises. As the Orthodox priest and author Alexander Schmemann expresses it:

'When man stands before the throne of God, when he has fulfilled all that God has given him to fulfil, when all sins are forgiven, all joy restored, then there is nothing else for him to do but give thanks. Eucharist (thanksgiving) is the state of perfect man. Eucharist is the life of paradise. Eucharist is the only full and real response of man to God's creation, redemption and gift of heaven. But this perfect man who stands before God is Christ. In him alone all that God has given man was fulfilled and brought back to heaven. He alone is the perfect eucharistic being. He is the eucharist of the world. In and through this eucharist the whole creation becomes what it always was to be and yet failed to be.' (52)

Worshipping God with heavenly company we are changed and so is the world weighing on our hearts. In pleading the memorial sacrifice of Christ's death and resurrection we are lifted into the heavenly hub of adoration. In communion with the Church in paradise and on earth we help effect the consecration of all that is to God's praise and service. This is a pointer to heaven. 'There light spills evermore from the fountain of light; it fills the creatures of God with God as much as they will contain, and yet enlarges their heart and vision to contain the more. There it is all one to serve and to pray, for God invisible is visibly portrayed in the action he inspires. There the flame of deity burns in the candle of mankind, Jesus Christ; and all the saints, united with him, extend his person, diversify his operation, and catch the running fire. That is the Church, the Israel of God, of which we only exist by being the colonies and outposts, far removed and fitfully aware; yet able by faith to annihilate both time and distance, and offer with them the only pleasing sacrifice to God Almighty, Father, Son and Holy Spirit; to him ascribing, as is most justly due, all might, dominion, majesty and power, henceforth and for ever. Amen.' (53)

NOTES

1   Malcolm Muggeridge, *Something Beautiful for God* (Harper Collins, 1972)

2   Brian Kolodiejchuk (Ed), *Mother Teresa – Come Be My Light* (Rider Books - 2008)

3   'There is a green hill far away' v4 (Cecil Frances Alexander 1818-95), Hymn 92, *New English Hymnal* (Canterbury Press, 1990)

4   Rupert Shortt, *God is No Thing* (Hurst & Company, 2016) p59

5   Apostles' Creed, *Common Worship: Services and Prayers for the Church of England* (The Archbishops' Council, 2000), p43

6   Thomas More quoted *Bible Alive*, August 2019, p45

7   John Twisleton, *Dynamical studies of crystalline polymers by inelastic neutron scattering,* (Oxford University D Phil thesis, 1973)

8   John Polkinghorne, *Quantum Physics & Theology – an unexpected kinship,* (SPCK, 2007)

9   John Twisleton, *Meet Jesus* (BRF, 2011), p29

10   Yesterday (2019), film directed by Danny Boyle, written by Richard Curtis, starring Himesh Patel

11   Thematic quotation from Anthony Bloom for 'Chaos and Beauty' Conference on the legacy of Metropolitan Anthony of Sourozh, October 26 2019

12   Pope Francis, *Lumen Fidei* (Vatican, 2013), Section 16

13   Fyodor Dostoevsky, *The Idiot* (Penguin Classics, 2004)

14   'For all the Saints' v5 (W. Walsham How 1823-97), Hymn 197, *New English Hymnal*

15   Blaise Pascal, *Thoughts* and *On the Art of Persuasion,* quoted *https://www.azquotes.com*

16   John Baker, *The Foolishness of God* (DLT, 1990)

17   Austin Farrer, *Said or Sung* (The Faith Press, 1960), *p165*

18   Westminster Abbey C.S.Lewis Memorial in Poets' Corner (2013)

19   Geoff Roberts and Anne Twisleton, *Mightier than the waves* (Geoff Roberts, 1981)

20   Quotations from the St Vincent de Paul Society of Australia website https://www.vinnies.org.au/page/About/History/Saint_Vincent_de_Paul/

21   Te Deum Laudamus vv8-12, *Common Worship: Daily Prayer* (Church House Publishing, 2005), p636

22   FJ Sheed (translator), *Collected Letters of St Therese of Lisieux* (Catholic Book Club, 1972), p167

23   John Donne, Izaak Walton & Andrew Motion (Preface), *Devotions upon emergent occasions and death's duel: With the life of Dr. John Donne by Izaak Walton* (Vintage, 1999 first published 1630)

24   Albert Camus, *The Myth of Sisyphus* (Penguin, 2013 first published 1942)

25   Timothy Keller, *The Reason for God* (Hodder & Stoughton, 2008), p25

26   'Lo! he comes with clouds descending' v3 (Charles Wesley 1707-88), Hymn 9, *New English Hymnal*

27   CS Lewis, *The Great Divorce* (Collins, 2012 first published 1945)

28   'My God loves me' v5 (Sandra Joan Billington), Hymn 499, *Celebration Hymnal for Everyone* (McCrimmons, 1994)

29   CS Lewis, *Mere Christianity* (Harper, 2001), pp 134-135.

30   Thomas Aquinas definition of faith, *Catechism of the Catholic Church* (Geoffrey Chapman, 1994), p39

31   Austin Farrer, *Saving Belief* (Hodder & Stoughton, 1964), p157

32.   Juliana Schmemann (translator), *The Journals of Father Alexander Schmemann 1973-1983* (St Vladimir's Seminary Press, 2000), p161

33   'Amazing grace' v3 (John Newton 1725-1807), Hymn 30, *Hymns Old & New* (Kevin Mayhew, 2004)

34   Apostles' Creed, *Common Worship,* p43

35   John Twisleton, *Experiencing Christ's Love* (BRF, 2017), p9-10

36   Justin Brierley, *Unbelievable?* (SPCK, 2017)

37   Austin Farrer, *Saving Belief*, p147

38   Richard Dawkins, *The God Delusion* (Bantam, 2006), p59

39   John Twisleton resurrection blog https://40resurrectionpointers.blogspot.com/

40   Wikipedia 2020, *The Resurrection of Jesus*

41   Tom Wright, *The Resurrection of the Son of God* (SPCK, 2003)

42   Peter Kreeft, *Love is stronger than death* (Ignatius Press, 1992)

43   Thornton Wilder, *The Bridge of San Luis Rey* (Longmans, 1929) p8

44   Bertrand Russell, *Autobiography, vol. 2* (Allen and Unwin, 1968), p159

45   Hermann Kohlbrugge quoted Kenneth Maas, *The John You Never Knew* (Peter Lang, 2006) p156

46   'All creatures of our God and King' v6 (St Francis of Assisi 1182-1226 translated by William Draper 1855-1933), Hymn 263, *New English Hymnal*

47   *Common Worship* p191-3

48   Andrew Wilson, *Spirit and Sacrament* (Zondervan, 2018), p45, p21

49   John Twisleton, *Meet Jesus* pp71-2

50   Second Vatican Council Constitution on the Sacred Liturgy n 83 in WM Abbott & J Gallagher *The Documents of Vatican II* (Geoffrey Chapman, 1966), p163

51   Report to Methodist Conference *Holy Communion in the Methodist Church* (2003) Note 77 p19

52   Alexander Schmemann, *The World as Sacrament* (DLT, 1965)

53   Austin Farrer *Said or Sung* p143

ABOUT THE AUTHOR

John Twisleton

John Twisleton is an ideas and people person, theologian and pastor, ministering as a priest in Brighton, UK. He broadcasts on London-based Premier Christian Radio and is well known as an author. His books include Meet Jesus (2011), Using the Jesus Prayer (2014) and Experiencing Christ's Love (2017).

BOOKS BY THIS AUTHOR

Forty Walks From Ally Pally

John Twisleton explores the byways of Haringey, Bsarnet and
Enfield with an eye to green spaces, local history and a replenish-
ment of the spirit. The routes, which vary in length between one
mile and twenty miles, exploit the public transport network, and
are well designed for family outings. The author provides here a
practical handbook for seeking space in North London.

Meet Jesus

In a world of competing philosophies, where does Jesus fit in?
How far can we trust the Bible and the Church? What difference does Jesus make to our lives and our communities? Is Jesus
really the be all and end all? John Twisleton provides a lively and
straightforward exploration of these and other questions pointing to how engaging with Jesus expands both mind and heart.

Firmly I Believe

Forty talks suited to Christians or non-Christians explaining
the creed, sacraments, commandment and prayer engaging with
misunderstandings and objections to faith and its practical expression. Double CD containing 40 easily digested 3 minute talks
accompanied by reflective music with full text in the accompanying booklet.

Using The Jesus Prayer

The Jesus Prayer of Eastern Orthodoxy, 'Lord Jesus Christ, Son of God, have mercy on me a sinner' offers a simple yet profound way of deepening spiritual life. John Twisleton gives practical guidance on how to use it outlining the simplification of life it offers.

Experiencing Christ's Love

A wake up call to the basic disciplines of worship, prayer, study, service and reflection helpful to loving God, neighbour and self. Against the backdrop of the message of God's love John Twisleton presents a rule of life suited to enter more fully the possibilities of God.

Empowering Priesthood

This book is an enthusiastic presentation about the gift and calling of the ministerial priesthood. It argues that the choosing and sending of priests is vital to the momentum of mission nd that their representation of Christ as priest, prophet and shepherd is given to help build love, consecrate in truth and bring empowerment to the whole priestly body of Christ.

Healing - Some Questions Answered

An examination of the healing ministry with suggested ecumenical forms for healing services. The booklet addresses divine intervention, credulity, lay involvement, evil spirits and the healing significance of the Eucharist

Christianity - Some Questions Answered

This booklet for Christian enquirers attempts dialogue between Chritianity and its contemporary critics. A brief inspection of

Christian faith clarifies both its unique claims and its universal wisdom so they can be seen and owned more fully.

Moorends And Its Church

Illustrated booklet telling the tale of the Doncaster suburb of Moorends from the sinking of the pit in 1904 to the 1984-5 mining dispute under the theme of death and resurrection. It includes a community survey of the needs of the elderly, young people and recreational and spiritual needs.

Holbrooks History

Illustrated booklet compiled by John Twisleton with members of St Luke's Church, Holbrooks in Coventry about their parish and its church. It describes a multicultural community that has welcomed Irish, West Indian, Eastern Europan and Indian workers ove the last century. The book includes dramatic pictures from the Second World War when the community and its church suffered bomb damage.

Entering The Prayer Of Jesus

Audio CD and booklet prepared by John Twisleton with the Diocese of Chichester and Premier Christian Radio providing spiritual wisdom from across the whole church. Contains audio contributions from Pete Greig (24-7 Prayer), Jane Holloway (Evangelical Alliance), Christopher Jamison (Worth Abbey), Molly Osborne (Lydia Fellowship) and Rowan Williams (Archbishop of Canterbury)

Baptism - Some Questions Answered

Illustrated booklet on infant baptism used across the Anglican Communion. It explains the commitments involved in baptising a baby, challenges hypocrisy and attempts to clear up a number of

misunderstandings in popular culture about what baptism is all about.

Confession - Some Questions Answered

Illustrated booklet explaining the value of sacramental confession as an aid to spiritual growth. It commends confession as a helpful discipline serving people as they struggle against sin and guilt and seek to renew church membership.

A History Of St Giles Church, Horsted Keynes

Besides being the burial place of former UK Prime Minister Harold MacMillan (1894-1986) and mystic ecumenist Archbishop Robert Leighton (1611-1684) St Giles, Horsted Keynes has association with the history of Sussex back to the 8th century. As 53rd Rector (2009-2017) John Twisleton wrote this illustrated history with the assistance of church members.

More At Twisleton.co.uk

Printed in Great Britain
by Amazon

85532575R00062